MAKING OF
MEDIEVAL
SPAIN

GABRIEL JACKSON

with 132 illustrations, 18 in colour

THAMES AND HUDSON · LONDON

For Kate and Rachel

Printed and bound in Great Britain by Jarrold and Sons Ltd, Norwich

ISBN 0 500 32023 3 *clothbound*
ISBN 0 500 33023 9 *paperbound*

CONTENTS

It has always seemed to me that by far the most significant aspect of Spanish medieval history was the constant interpenetration of the three distinctive cultures present in the peninsula: the Islamic, the Hebrew and the Christian. Nowhere else in the world has there been such prolonged struggle, such symbiosis and such mutual influence among the three great religious traditions of the Western World. In a brief work one must inevitably slight many important topics, and I have consciously chosen to treat cultural questions at the expense of detailed political and diplomatic history. I have also sought to narrate side by side the main developments in Islamic and Christian Spain rather than to write what would amount to separate 'national' histories of the two halves of medieval Spain.

Much of my research was done on a Fellowship from the American Council of Learned Societies during the academic year 1967–68; and a grant from the Humanities Institute gave me much-needed writing time during the summer of 1970. I owe many important ideas and bibliographical suggestions to several colleagues: J. M. Lacarra of the University of Saragossa, C. J. Bishko of the University of Virginia, William Watson of MIT, and Guillermo Céspedes and James T. Monroe of the University of California at San Diego.

September 1970
La Jolla, California

I THE CENTURIES OF ISLAMIC DOMINION

The Islamic occupation of Spain occurred with puzzling rapidity. Between 711 and 718 several incompletely co-ordinated expeditions, numbering no more than twenty-five thousand soldiers in all, managed with very few pitched battles to conquer all but the most mountainous north-western portions of the peninsula. Neither the military nor the political details are entirely clear, but the main outlines can be reconstructed from the partial evidence. The Visigothic monarchy had for decades been undermined by family rivalries. To a large proportion of the Spanish population the king Roderic who was killed at Guadalete was in fact a usurper, and the North African invaders had come at the request of the partisans of the legitimate claimant Aquila. In addition, the monarchy had never achieved complete religious or political unity.

In general the Levantine and Andalusian populations which had been the most completely romanized, and which had also been the most deeply influenced by Byzantine rule, were Athanasian (Trinitarian) Christians, and were accustomed to the concept of a hereditary, authoritarian kingship. According to Visigothic tradition, kingship was in principle elective, although considerable efforts had been made to establish a hereditary succession. Until the spectacular conversion of Reccared in 587 the rulers had been Arian (Unitarian) Christians, and, while officially all Spain had become Athanasian during the seventh century, the Arian undercurrent remained strong, associated as it was with the national heritage of the Visigoths. Politically speaking, neither Suevian resistance in Galicia nor Basque resistance in the Pyrenees, nor the independent spirit of the oldest Hispano-Roman towns in Andalusia and the Levant had ever been completely eliminated.

9

1   Dedicatory crown of the Visigothic king Recceswinth, 653–72; set in gold, the crown is formed of sapphires, pearls, agates and rock-crystals.

For legal and administrative authority the Visigothic kings depended upon the aid of church councils, and the bishops who constituted these councils of course had personal and family ambitions of their own. There seems also to have been a marked increase in the persecution of the Jews, who formed a major segment of the merchant and artisan classes. Thus when the caliph of Damascus was invited to intervene in Spain his troops were welcomed by a large proportion of both the ruling aristocracy and the Jews; and most of the Hispano-Roman rural and urban population felt neither the loyalty to a united monarchy nor the strong religious unity which might have created a type of national resistance to the Islamic invader.

The troops of Tariq and Musa rapidly occupied the main towns of Andalusia. During the ensuing seven years, as much by diplomacy as by battle, they brought the whole peninsula under their control except for the most mountainous areas where the population was thin and little wealth was to be found. Ignoring Asturias and most of Galicia during the 720s they attempted rather to extend their occupation to southern France. The turning-point of their military advance came in 732 with their defeat near Poitiers by Charles Martel, but they continued to make occasional raids on the Mediterranean coastal towns of France throughout the eighth century.

The rapidity of the Islamic conquest should probably be attributed principally to the disunity of the Visigothic rulers and to the indifference if not the hostility of the mass of the Hispano-Roman population. The invaders themselves made no attempt to revolutionize the society which they found. The Hispano-Roman towns, even in relative decay, and the great agricultural estates of the Visigothic nobility were more prosperous than those of the Maghrib. The Visigothic supporters of the invasion retained their estates; the expropriated lands of the partisans of Roderic were distributed to Islamic war captains who made no immediate changes in the system of cultivation, and who appear to have courted the local population by somewhat improving the conditions of share-cropping. Little propaganda and no force were employed to obtain religious conversions. The majority of the North African troops were semi-pagan, and the Arab leaders, who in the preceding half century had already occupied many lands with large Christian populations, were specifically tolerant of all 'Peoples of the Book', i.e. Jews and Christians whose revealed religion and holy writings were respected as the forerunners of the final revelation: that of Allah to his prophet Muhammad.

The Islamic invaders themselves were by no means thoroughly united. Within the ruling group, Arabs, Syrians and Egyptians were mutually suspicious, and none of them could be sure of the loyalty of their largely Berber troops. More than one overly ambitious war captain was executed for exceeding orders. No fewer than twenty-three governors of Spain were named by the caliph between 732 and 755. It took an average of four months to travel between Damascus and Seville or Cordoba, and the lines of communication were constantly being threatened by local revolts in North Africa. Within the peninsula, rival ethnic groups established themselves in chosen areas: the Arabs in the Guadalquivir valley, the Syrians in Granada, the Egyptians in Murcia, the Berbers in the hill country of Andalusia and the high plains of Extremadura and central Spain. The invaders everywhere occupied the best land and the positions of command, but except for the Berbers their actual numbers were negligible. A fierce spirit of local autonomy developed, combining the rivalries of the invading élites with the long-standing spirit of local sovereignty which had limited the effectiveness of both Roman and Visigothic rule. A severe famine in central Spain in about 750 sent thousands of Berber immigrants back to Africa.

Yet at no time in these forty years of civil broils and administrative confusion was there ever any question of reversing the Islamic conquest. The overthrow of the Umayyad caliphate in Damascus, and its replacement by the rule of the Abbasids, contributed indirectly to the beginnings of a slightly more stable political system in Spain. In the year 756 a very able young

2 Visigothic gold *solidus*, modelled on contemporary Byzantine *solidii*; left, 'portrait' of king Wamba (672–80) and, right, the characteristic Byzantine motif of a cross on steps.

Umayyad prince who had miraculously survived the slaughter of his family in Syria arrived in Spain, along with a few advisers who had had military and political experience under the Umayyads. Abd-al-Rahman I (756–88) must have possessed considerable personal magnetism in order to turn the dubious advantage of his lineage into a tangible political asset. Successfully playing off against each other several strong local régimes, and combining the 'legitimacy' of his claim with the offer of virtual Spanish independence under an Umayyad régime which would resist the centralizing demands of the Abbasid caliph, he established the emirate of Cordoba, choosing his capital for its central location in relation to the main cities of Islamic Spain, its rich agricultural hinterland, and perhaps also for its relatively small Christian population.

Although his reign was at no time completely free of local revolts, he was able to found a central administration which in one form or another was to function for two and a half centuries. By the time of his death in 788, he controlled all of eastern Hispania south of the Pyrenees except for Navarre. Towards the west his effective sovereignty covered all the lands south of the Duero river. As far as possible he preferred a policy of tolerance towards all ethnic and religious groups, and sought to reconcile those who had exercised power during the anarchic decades

3 Interior of the sanctuary of the Great Mosque, Cordoba: the double horseshoe arches, in contrasting colours and materials, are a typical element of the Spanish-Arab architectural style. ▶

prior to 756. He could be utterly ruthless when conciliation failed. Thus, after defeating a pro-Abbasid rebellion in 763, he sent the salted and camphored heads of the executed leaders to Damascus, where the caliph Chafar al-Mansur is said to have expressed his immense relief at the presence of a broad sea between him and the Umayyad emir.

By the close of his reign Abd-al-Rahman had developed a professional army numbering perhaps 40,000, officered by Syrians and Berbers, and recruited mostly among Berbers in North Africa and Slavs imported from eastern Europe. He had established economic independence of Damascus by adopting the Roman weights and measures which were traditional in Hispanic commerce, and by coining his own gold dinars. We have no trade statistics for the eighth century, but Cordoba must have played a dominant role in commercial relations with Europe, inasmuch as the Carolingian financial system was re-formed in 780 on the basis of a coin weighing precisely half the Cordoban dinar. Abd-al-Rahman also began the construction of the Great Mosque of Cordoba, and in 785 the latter had a capacity of 5,500 worshippers.

From the time of the conquest until almost the end of the eighth century, Christian Spain was confined to two nuclei, a small rural kingdom in the Asturian mountains and an even smaller Basque realm in the vicinity of Pamplona. The first kings of Asturias and Navarre were wealthy cattlemen who doubled as guerrilla war captains. They had no regular administration or army. They used Cordoban, Byzantine, or Carolingian coins as standards of value, but did all their actual trading in barter. Literacy was confined to a minority of the priesthood, and the only literary culture was the study of the Roman and Visigothic church fathers. Alfonso I of Asturias (739–57) created, as a matter of policy, a broad no-man's-land between himself and Islamic Spain. The population of old Roman cities such as Tuy, Astorga and Leon was deliberately transferred north of the Cantabrican mountains. Theoretically the Hispanic church remained united under the aegis of the metropolitan of

14

4 Decorated multifoil archway in the Great Mosque, Cordoba, begun in 785, and converted after the Reconquest into a cathedral. ▶

5 Charlemagne, portrayed as judge and soldier on a late ninth-century bronze figure.

6 Alfonso II at prayer with his armour-bearer: from a twelfth-century illuminated manuscript. ▶

Toledo, but the Asturian monarchy chafed at subordination to a church hierarchy which was itself under Muslim rule, and the Adoptionist controversy (a sequel to the old Arian heresy) gave Alfonso II (791–842) the opportunity in 795 to declare his ecclesiastical independence of the captive Visigothic church.

Meanwhile, the Carolingian empire was tentatively expanding across the Pyrenees. An expedition to Saragossa in 778 led to disaster, both for the Christians within the city who had risen at the approach of the Carolingian army and for that army itself, whose retreat was ambushed in the Pyrenees by the Navarrese, who objected to the pretensions of Charlemagne as much as to those of the emir. Both banks of the Ebro were to remain under Islamic control for two more centuries, but small Frankish domains were established in Upper Catalonia and in the high

ADEFONS REX CASTVS

A RMIGER REGIS

Pyrenean valleys: Gerona, 785; Urgel, 789; Pallars and Ribagorza, c. 808; and Barcelona by 812. Together these small counties constituted the 'Spanish March' of the Carolingian empire. Being far from the centre of Frankish power, and living on an exposed frontier, they enjoyed considerable autonomy. Thus the emperor Charlemagne granted exceptional privileges to Barcelona: military service only under their own count; their own judges except for murder, kidnapping and arson; no quartering of royal officials except the occasional *missi*; homage to the count without any accompanying tax or tribute. These privileges were the effective beginning of a long tradition of independence in the internal government of Catalonia. At the same time the priesthood in all these counties was attached to the archbishopric of Narbonne, and changes in French monastic organization were applied to the Spanish March. Thus culturally and politically nascent Catalonia was drawn into the French orbit while Navarre and Asturias maintained their independence – and their more primitive character.

7   Spain at the beginning of the ninth century.

8 Charlemagne invests Roland with the Spanish March: from a twelfth-century manuscript.

During the ninth and tenth centuries the emirate (and after 929 the caliphate) of Cordoba was clearly the dominant society in the Hispanic peninsula. That society was characterized by a unique blend of economic prosperity, able administration, arbitrary and often cruel political practices, religious and racial tolerance, and constant tension involving Oriental and Hispanic cultural influences. The prosperity of al-Andalus, as it came to be known, was based upon a varied combination of agriculture, industry and trade. To speak first of agriculture: the new rulers made only the most minimal changes in landownership, simply displacing a portion of the Visigothic aristocracy with their own war captains. But whereas under the Visigoths the peasants had been virtual slaves, and had owed anything from 50 to 80 per cent of their crops to their landlords, the Muslims treated peasants as free men, and exacted only 20 to 50 per cent of the produce.

Quite as important as the more favourable share-cropping arrangements was the attitude towards the land. The Arabs, who had come out of the desert, were great lovers of water, of gardens and of trees. They and their North African followers

19

appreciated, in the river valleys of Andalusia, the kind of climate which in their homelands could be found only in occasional oases. The generation of the conquerors were, for the most part, men of less culture than the Hispano-Romans who had suddenly become their subjects. During the course of the ninth and tenth centuries the Andalusian ruling class increasingly adopted both the aesthetic and the economic practices of the Middle East, which was the heartland of Muslim civilization. Wheat was the basic food crop, and while there were occasional local famines due to war or insect plagues, Islamic Spain generally produced a grain surplus. Olive cultivation and forests were more extensive than at any other time in peninsular history. From the Orient citrus fruits, peaches, bananas, almonds and figs were introduced; likewise important commercial crops such as cotton, silk, saffron, esparto, flax, hemp and wool. At the same time, though no obedient Muslim would eat pork, pigs continued to be raised in most of the same areas as during Roman and Visigothic times.

9   Santiago de Peñalba: consecrated in 931, this church served as a sanctuary for Mozarabic monks leaving al-Andalus.

20

The Prophet had loved pigeons and bees, and his example was followed by even the most modest Andalusian farmers. The donkey, originally imported from Egypt, greatly increased the productive capacity of its master. Middle Eastern and Egyptian improvements in irrigation were rapidly adopted, as was the use of trees for aesthetic purposes. The Spanish Muslims valued both the economic and aesthetic use of all elements of the natural environment, as is witnessed by the care with which houses and windows were located for the greatest possible benefit from the view. It would be going too far to say that the Spanish Muslims loved nature with the same self-conscious intensity as did the nineteenth-century European romantics, but most certainly they prized the possibilities of their environment.

Considerable industrial development also took place during the ninth and tenth centuries: ceramics, utensils and decorative ware in all metals, leather goods, ivory work, furniture and perfumes were produced by thousands of artisans working

21

11, 12   Carved ivory box
made   for   Almoqueira,
prince of Cordoba, in 967.

individually or in very small groups in the several dozen cities
of Islamic Spain. Business organization on a larger scale was
involved in the production of textiles, tapestries, arms and dyes.
Flint glass was a ninth-century Cordoban invention, and mines,
exploited by individual capitalists rather than by the state as in
Roman times, produced iron, mercury and rock-salt. Trade increased steadily, and, so far as we know, was little interrupted by
the almost constant civil wars of al-Andalus or the frontier
skirmishes with the Christians. Muslim Spain exported textiles,
olive oil and arms to North Africa, in return for which it possessed a virtual monopoly of the European imports of Sudanese
gold. This bullion in turn supported the vast building pro-
grammes and the steady growth of the Cordoban standing
army. Oil and gold were exported to the Middle East, in exchange for which Spain received spices, artisan wares and
fabrics. Christian Spain was at first a small market, but it became, by the later tenth century at least, the principal market
both for Andalusian industry and for the re-export of Oriental
luxuries.

22

13 Above, detail from the tenth-century 'Veil of Hisham', of silk and gold. The inscription bears the name of Hisham II (976–1009).

14 Right, earthenware wine-jar, with grapevine design incised in the clay.

23

Spain also played a part in international trade in Carolingian times. In particular the trade in east European slaves, often the captives of Frankish armies, passed overland through Christian Spain, contributing heavily to the growth of Barcelona and slightly to that of Pamplona. Slavery, then as now, seems to have made invidious distinctions based upon colour. In the early tenth century an accomplished black girl might be sold for anything from 150 to 300 dinars. An uneducated white slave would cost 1,000 dinars. The most expensive slaves were fine artisans and singers, who in rare cases could bring over 10,000 dinars. Carolingian France stood in awe of the variety and splendour of the Cordoban economy. The Muslim world was also impressed. Ninth- and tenth-century travellers from Egypt and the Maghrib remarked upon the prosperity and independent spirit of Spanish artisans, the relative absence of poverty and the high proportion of labour-saving donkeys and of horses.

Administratively speaking, Muslim Spain was divided into about thirty units, with special and frequently changing classifications for those bordering the Christian north. The varied economy, and the great importance of trade, meant that the cities governed the countryside, as they had during the first centuries of the Roman empire, in contrast with the rural-dominated feudal system which was developing at the same time in neighbouring France. Provincial governors were appointed and removed at the pleasure of the emir. Generally, they were chosen from distinguished families, especially in the frontier districts, but the emirs attempted to prevent the growth of any sort of hereditary governing caste, and they availed themselves of talent without regard to ethnic background. Ancestry, however, was not unimportant. Especially during the ninth century, when Oriental influences were consciously imported, Arab and Syrian ancestry had considerable prestige – so much so that many ambitious Hispano-Muslims forged Arab pedigrees for themselves. But the emirs, so far as they were able, kept all high government careers 'open to talent' and to their arbitrary power of appointment.

The emir also had an advisory cabinet, composed of about a dozen viziers specializing in such matters as finance, trade, justice, diplomacy and war. They too were appointed at pleasure, but were not expected to be yes-men. The officials with the most independence, however, were the cadis – the municipal judges who heard personal, property, commercial and tax cases of all sorts. They were chosen for their learning and their personal integrity; they often possessed life tenure in fact if not in law; and they were able to protect the ordinary subject from the worst exactions of landlords, merchants and high officials.

The maintenance of honesty in coinage, weights and measures, the renting of market-stalls and warehouse space also depended principally upon the cadis. The proportion of non-Muslims in the population was probably higher than in any other part of the Islamic world. In accordance with Muslim tradition, the Christian and Jewish communities retained their own organization under their own priests and rabbis. They had separate law courts for their family and business affairs. They controlled their own religious buildings and community schools. The special lump-sum taxes which were levied on all non-Muslims in lieu of military service were apportioned within the communities and collected by their own officers.

Although there was much able administration, especially at the municipal level, the basic political system was extremely arbitrary and unstable. The emirs tended to accumulate all supreme political and religious authority in their own hands, and after 929 the caliphate was openly caesaro-papist in nature. Islam, like Christianity, bred heresies from the very beginning, and these heresies frequently implied a challenge to political as well as spiritual authority. The emir Hisham I (788–96) adopted Malikite orthodoxy as the official doctrine of Islamic Spain. The eminent Arabian jurist Malik Ibn Anas had been an outspoken opponent of all philosophical and religious speculations. He aggressively advocated 'strict construction' of the Koran and of the Prophet's sayings and established a conservative,

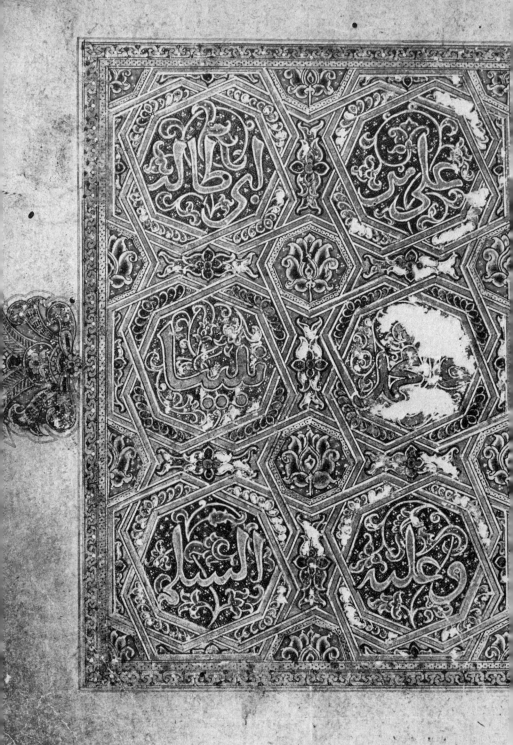

anti-rational and anti-speculative tradition which was used by Hisham and all his successors as a means to buttress royal authority. The dominance of the official Malikite orthodoxy may have had as one of its by-products the relative poverty of Islamic philosophical literature in Spain itself.

Succession to the emirate, in contrast with all other high offices, was hereditary, but without any significant emphasis on primogeniture. The emir tried, in principle, to arrange for the succession of his ablest son, but his decisions were much complicated by the practice of polygamy. Islamic law permitted a man to have four official wives and as many unofficial concubines as he could afford. In the highly developed urban society of al-Andalus, polygamy was a form of 'conspicuous consumption' engaged in only by the highest ranks of the aristocracy. But most of the emirs had several dozen children by any number of mothers. Much of the energy of viziers was taken up in either placating or exploiting ferocious inner family rivalries, and eunuchs became important as spies, guardians and go-betweens in harem politics.

Leaf from a
an painted in
it 1000.

16   Detail of an ivory casket of about 970 showing a person of rank travelling in state, one of the relatively few examples in Muslim art of the piction of human life.

From Arab literary sources we can derive a fairly detailed picture of the personal and political influences surrounding the emir Abd-al-Rahman II (822–52), who was a ruler of great intelligence, a builder, aesthete and conscious imitator of the culture of the Baghdad caliphate. In the first year of his reign he eagerly welcomed to Cordoba the distinguished poet and musician Ziryab, who had been exiled from Baghdad. Ziryab brought with him a knowledge of Oriental cuisine, perfumes, cosmetics and silk clothes which had been hitherto almost unknown on the relatively crude western frontier of Islam. As the emir's chief adviser in cultural matters he also introduced the Oriental style of protocol whereby the sovereign might be seen only by his leading subjects. His patronage was instrumental in the adoption of crystal goblets (invented in Spain), in place of the gold and silver goblets which had been previously used at state banquets. He also established the order of the menu: soup, to be followed by meat, and then by sweets. His musical and poetic style set the artistic tone in Cordoba for thirty-five years until his death in 857, and as the emir's confidant he enjoyed the right of access to the royal apartments through a secret entrance.

17 Rock-crystal chalice of probable Muslim origin: the chalice itself has been incorporated into a design of later date.

18 The tower of San Juan, Cordoba, dating from the reign of Abd-al-Rahman II, was originally a minaret, the mosque being later converted into a church.

Probably the most important single political figure at the court of Abd-al-Rahman II was the Hispano-Muslim eunuch Abu-l-Fath Nasr, who had played a leading role in the defence of Seville against Norman raiders in 844. Nasr went on to become the *de facto* head of the entire palace administration, the man whose word was essential to anyone wishing directly to influence the emir. A third figure of key importance was the emir's favourite mistress Tarub, upon whom he showered expensive gifts and to whom he addressed highly flattering if not very imaginative poems. There were at least six other concubines who exercised a degree of personal influence over him, as well as having provided him with sons. But Tarub seems to have enjoyed a special ascendancy. She was apparently not able, however, to convince him that he should declare as heir to the throne her son rather than an older prince by another mother. In desperation she attempted, in co-operation with Nasr, to poison the emir and the presumptive heir Muhammad. Abd-al-Rahman was warned in time, and obliged Nasr to drink the poisoned draught which his chief administrator had offered him as a supposedly medicinal drink. According to the Arab chronicles, Tarub herself was not punished, and in fact plotted unsuccessfully once more to place her son on the throne during the last days of the emir's lingering illness.

A fourth personality of great influence during the early years of the reign was the orthodox theologian Yahya ibn Yahya. The latter had in fact fomented religious revolts during the reign of al-Hakam I (796–822). Neither judges nor religious councillors at the court could be named without the approval of Yahya, and his constant criticism of public officials was apparently largely responsible for the fact that during a thirty-year reign no less than eleven cadis were named in Cordoba – the office of cadi was generally held for long periods by men of established prestige. It will always be arguable, on the basis of the slender documentary evidence available, exactly how influential particular concubines or theologians, eunuchs or poets were. What is perfectly clear is the arbitrary nature of power at the top in the Hispano-Muslim government. It could be exercised directly by a strong emir, and by his freely designated representatives, for exactly as long as those representatives enjoyed his favour. And in the case of weak sovereigns, a strong prince or palace official, whether a free man or a slave, would exercise equally arbitrary power in the name of the emir.

The Christians of the north, the great nineteenth-century historians such as Reinhard Dozy and Ignace Goldziher, and contemporary students of Muslim Spain, have all been fascinated by the combination of high culture and political instability characteristic of the Muslim states. The emirs patronized, with discriminating judgment, all aspects of the arts and of technology. They were tolerant and supple in relation to the large Mozarabic (Christian) and Jewish communities in their cities. They were sophisticated in their diplomatic and trade relations with Europe, Byzantium and North Africa. As in all wealthy societies of the pre-industrial era, they exploited large numbers of slaves; however, talented slaves could exercise the highest administrative, artistic and scientific functions, and the emirs were far less prejudiced in religious and ethnic matters than are most of the rulers in the world today.

At the same time absolute political and religious power, and the opportunity (by no means always indulged) for unrestrained sensuality, made for arbitrary, and often cruel, political practices. Sadism, torture and assassination were normal political methods, often referred to with some pride in poems attributed to various rulers, and certainly mentioned without any sense of shock in all the Arab histories.

The emirate was constantly beset by conflicts between Cordoba and the outlying cities, and between ethnic élites and the Hispanic population. In the entire period of the emirate (756–929) scarcely twenty years passed without a major military revolt. The principal foci of discontent were the frontier cities of Merida, Toledo and Saragossa, and the coastal ports: Malaga, Almeria, Murcia. And conflicts which involved native Spanish resentment against Arabs or Syrians or Egyptians might very well come to involve the Christian population as natural allies, in such cases, of their Hispano-Muslim cousins. In the two and a half centuries following the conquest, a solid majority of the population south of the Duero and Ebro rivers became Muslim. Indeed, one of the better documented revolts of the ninth century, that of the Mozarabs of Cordoba (c. 850–59), was caused in large measure by the despair with which an educated minority of the Mozarabs witnessed the steady religious and cultural attrition of their community. Although Christians and Jews were free to worship as they saw fit, public insults to Allah were punishable by death. A small group of Mozarabs decided deliberately to court death by publicly denigrating the Prophet. The emir was reluctant to impose the death penalty, but was forced to do so by the fanatical reaction of the urban Muslim masses and by the open challenge to his political and religious authority. The bishop of Cordoba defended the martyrs, but the

Mozarabic church hierarchy as a whole opposed the movement as contrary to the interest of the Christian community. And the reign of Muhammad I (852–86) witnessed the mass conversion of the Cordoban Christians following the failure of the martyr movement.

The limits on Islamic control of Spain became perfectly clear during the ninth century. The population remained bilingual, with Romance the family language even of the great majority of Muslims. Though the number of Christians declined, the remaining ones were largely bourgeois and artisans whose functions gave them greater influence than their numbers alone would warrant. Christians and Hispano-Muslims made common cause to resist the orientalization of both culture and politics. The emir Abd-al-Rahman III (912–61) spent the first twenty years of his reign putting down persistent local revolts. When he declared himself caliph in 929 he was at least partly motivated by the urgent need to hispanize his rule in order to reconcile his own Muslim subjects.

During the ninth and tenth centuries the steady increase of population in both Muslim and Christian Spain resulted in increasing attention, both peaceful and warlike, being paid to the relatively unpopulated frontier districts. Without really challenging the over-all economic and cultural supremacy of Cordoba, the Christian kingdoms nevertheless registered substantial advances in power, population, self-conscious dignity and long-range purpose. In the 740s Alfonso I of Asturias had purposely withdrawn the population from the upper Duero valley to the Cantabrican mountains. A century later Ordoño I (850–66) and Alfonso III (866–910) repopulated a series of important towns along the line of the Duero and Arlanzon valleys: Tuy, Astorga, Orete and Amaya in 854, Leon in 856, Cea in 875, Coimbra and Sahagun in 880, Burgos in 884, Zamora in 893 and Toro in 900. In Leon and Astorga Mozarabic artisans emigrating from al-Andalus co-operated with Galician and Asturian mountaineers in the repair of many still surviving Roman houses. Along the Duero and its tributaries free peasants

32

19 Ordoño I. A 'portrait' from a twelfth-century illuminated manuscript. ▶

ORDONIUS REX . PRIMUS :

rdonius rex tibi patri nro ataulfo epo
mittimus tibi per hanc nram precepcionē
nros pueros et familiares numeros qui pro
reuerencia et honore beatissimi iacobi

20 The Arca Santa (shrine) of Alfonso III. The casket, made in 1075, is of cedar-wood, silver-gilt plated and inlaid with coloured paste, and is decorated with scenes from the life of Christ, the Virgin Mary and the Apostles.

obtained land from the king by means of *presura*, i.e. gaining clear title in return for clearing, ploughing and raising crops. Hastening to protect their own frontiers, the Muslim rulers in the 860s founded or repopulated the towns of Madrid, Salamanca, Badajoz, Tudela and Calatrava. In the Christian interior political conditions became sufficiently stable, and the rural economy sufficiently prosperous, to support large family domains and monasteries in Galicia and Asturias. The Visigothic ecclesiastical tradition was maintained by monks who preserved, and wrote new commentaries on, the works of Isidore of Seville. At the same time they established their independence of both Toledo and Rome by intensive development of the cult of Santiago following the presumed discovery, sometime in the 820s, of the tomb of St James the Greater in a field near what later became the city of Santiago de Compostela.

34

21 St James of Compostela. A twelfth-century statue of the saint displays the pilgrim's staff and scallop shell, symbol of pilgrimage. ▶

22   The castle at Peñafiel, built in the eleventh century and reconstructed in 1307.

Almost imperceptibly a significant social difference began to evolve between the north-western provinces of Leon, Asturias and Galicia on the one hand, and the small county of Castile on the other. Along the western stretches of the Duero, and in the territory to the north of it, the population remained thin so that hostile contact with the Muslims was only sporadic. But along the Arlanzon, near Burgos, and along the upper Ebro, near Miranda and Haro, contact with Islamic Spain was constant. The upper Ebro was populated by prosperous Muslim farmers under the sovereignty of the Banu Qasi of Saragossa, and the river valley itself was the favoured invasion route for Muslim raiding parties. Neither large agricultural estates nor heavily endowed monasteries were established in this area; nor did Mozarabic artisans and scholarly priests settle there. The warlike frontier of early medieval Spain was a miniature 'wild west', attractive to adventurous, combative men who were willing to live dangerously and uncomfortably rather than submit to established hierarchies. The area was dotted with castles, from which eventually came the name Castile. The people who re-settled it were the dour mountaineers of the Basque country, those who had most fiercely resisted romanization, and had later fought the Visigoths and the Franks in order to maintain their independence. As small farmers staking out their claims against the authority of both Leon and Cordoba, they owed fealty only to their local counts.

Little touched by either Mozarabic or Latin culture, they created the folk-poetry which placed its special stamp on the entire growth of the Castilian language. A large body of that folk-poetry offers a legendary version of the career of a militarily and maritally impressive adventurer named Fernan Gonzalez. Legend has made him the virtual founder of Castile, and the great exemplar, along with the Cid, of its specific virtues. Historical investigation has considerably reduced both his practical importance and his moral stature, but the relatively sketchy outlines of his actual career are very instructive for understanding the politics of tenth-century Spain.

23 The construction of castles continued throughout the Middle Ages: shown below is Manzanares el Real, built in the fifteenth century for the Mendoza family.

Fernan Gonzalez' father was one of several local chieftains who had established their titles as 'count' by founding a frontier city, in this case the town of Lara. He died in 916, and Fernan's mother successfully held on to his castle and his legal claims until her young son came of age. In 929 Fernan Gonzalez became the legally recognized count of Lara. At about this time he made a politically very advantageous marriage to Sancha, one of the daughters of queen Toda of Navarre, and the widow of the late king Ordoño II of Leon. During the 930s he was one of the favoured war captains of Ramiro II of Leon (931–51), and held the title of count of Castile in return for his services and the royal favour. In about 940 he apparently quarrelled with Ramiro over his ambition likewise to be named count of Monzon. The title went to a rival family, the Ansurez. Allying himself with another dissatisfied count, Diego Muñoz of Saldaña, he revolted against Ramiro in 943, was captured and imprisoned; in 945 he was freed, but only upon his oath of fidelity accompanied by the surrender of his tenancies. In some manner, however, the new count of Castile must have made himself unpopular, and by 947 Fernan Gonzalez had been restored to his old titles; to cement the family alliance he gave his daughter Urraca in marriage to Ramiro's heir, thereby becoming the father-in-law of the future Ordoño III (951–56).

His position as the most powerful political adviser, and perhaps also as the wealthiest landed magnate of Leon, aroused the jealousy of his mother-in-law queen Toda, and the royal quarrels which disastrously weakened the kingdom of Leon after 951 can only be understood in the light of complicated family rivalries. Ramiro II had had two sons by different wives: Ordoño, whose mother was a Galician princess, and Sancho, whose mother was Urraca, daughter of Toda. Since Ordoño of the Galician mother had married Fernan Gonzalez' daughter (also named Urraca) it must have seemed in 951 as though the ambitious Castilian count would dominate Leon, perhaps to the exclusion of Navarrese influence. Relations between Ordoño, his wife and his father-in-law were not good during the brief reign, and neither Fernan Gonzalez nor his daughter spent much time in Leon; when Ordoño III died unexpectedly in 956 he left no heir.

This death gave Toda her long-awaited opportunity to re-establish Navarrese influence in Leon. Ramiro's second son Sancho, the logical but not the uncontested candidate for the throne, was her grandson. Fernan Gonzalez attempted to check the designs of his mother-in-law by promptly marrying his widowed daughter to a cousin of the late king, whom he then tried to impose on the Galician and Leonese nobility as Ordoño IV. Queen Toda now formed a coalition against him consisting of Navarre, Cordoba, the Ansurez family (rival counts of Castile) and a large proportion of the Leonese nobility. In 959 he was simultaneously attacked by Cordoban troops from the south and Navarrese troops from the east. Captured and imprisoned in Pamplona, he was freed upon signing a new pact with the formidable queen, whereby he agreed to help her grandson, prince Sancho (son of Ramiro II), to establish himself as king of Leon, a move which of course meant repudiation of his new son-in-law, Ordoño IV. Meanwhile his wife (Sancha, daughter of Toda) had died, and he promptly married another Navarrese heiress, Urraca, daughter of king Garcia Sanchez. In 962 his disgraced son-in-law Ordoño died in Cordoba, where the caliph had received him condescendingly and pigeon-holed his request for military aid in an effort to regain the Leonese throne. Fernan Gonzalez, always the solicitous father, now married his daughter Urraca (widow of Ordoños III and IV) to prince Sancho Abarca, the heir to the throne of Navarre. At the time of his death, about 970, he could look back upon a highly adventurous life in which he had twice quarrelled and been reconciled with reigning kings, twice made advantageous marriages for himself, and had managed to marry his daughter successively to three royal heirs of Leon and Navarre.

The roles of queen Toda and of the caliphate are also instructive in relation to the history of tenth-century Castile and its legendary count. Toda, queen mother of Navarre, always overshadowed her son, king Garcia Sanchez, and was the key political figure in Christian Spain during the decades between 930 and 970. Her daughters were the wives of leading Galician and Asturian princes. Besides being the mother-in-law of Fernan Gonzalez, she was also the great aunt of the caliph Abd-al-Rahman III and the grandmother of Sancho, younger son of Ramiro II, who suddenly found himself heir to the throne upon the death of Ordoño III in 956. She was unable immediately to have Sancho recognized as king, however, for among other reasons the unfortunate youth was so obese that he was unable to mount a horse, let alone manage a throne amidst athletic and not very docile subjects. Toda appealed to her great-nephew, the caliph, asking whether his personal physician, the internationally famous Hasday ben Shaprut, would consent to treat the prince. Hasday, who was also a great linguist and diplomat, reputedly fluent in Arabic, Hebrew, Greek and Romance, came to Pamplona on a mission from his sovereign. He imposed humiliating conditions on the queen; namely that the patient would have to come to Cordoba for treatment, and that Leon would have to yield several frontier castles. She accepted, however, and spent some months in Cordoba during 958. While Hasday employed a vegetarian diet to reduce the fat grandson, she forged the military alliance which defeated Fernan Gonzalez and placed Sancho on the throne of Leon in 959.

Our specific knowledge of all the persons referred to in these paragraphs is based upon a handful of legal documents, and sparse personal references in Leonese and Cordoban chronicles. But certain aspects of tenth-century society are abundantly clear. The northern kingdoms, and the newly founded counties, were governed as family properties. Marital alliances played a great role, and bitter quarrels among cousins and in-laws resulted partly from the fact that primogeniture was not consistently followed, and partly from the fact that not even a rudimentary 'administration' existed to smooth over transitional periods and to strengthen the hand of weak princes.

24 The importance of marital alliances. Here a lord transmits feudal rights by giving his daughter in marriage, with the approval of his wife.

Strong women could hold property and offices on behalf of their sons, and their political influence was evidently not limited by their sex. Cordoba dominated the peninsula culturally, and was the strongest single military power, but Christian coalitions under an able king such as Ramiro II could contain, and occasionally defeat, Cordoban armies. The caliph was frequently the arbiter of quarrels among the Christian kingdoms. From the evidence of both intermarriage and diplomacy it would seem that religious antagonism played only the smallest role in political alignments.

Cordoban domination of the peninsula in the tenth century rested squarely on her diversified economy, which continued to flourish and develop along lines already described. Neither political instability, nor African and Christian challenges, adversely affected that economy, since in terms of population, volume of trade, naval and military efficiency and prestige (as measured by embassies and by the international importance of Cordoban coinage) the caliphate represented the apogee of Islamic power in Spain. Yet Cordoba, despite her economic wealth and her highly developed administrative system, did not achieve true political stability. Thus Abd-al-Rahman III was obliged to spend the first twenty years of his reign subduing revolts in the mountains of Andalusia and in the always restive frontier provinces of Merida, Toledo and Saragossa. After he had achieved firm physical control of his domains, he attempted once and for all to end the power of the great Arab families whose prestige had been developed a century earlier under the orientalizing emir Abd-al-Rahman II. Abd-al-Rahman III announced his full independence of Baghdad by assuming the title of caliph in 929. He substituted Spaniards and Slavs for officials of Oriental descent, a move which helped him simultaneously to reduce the role of the Arab aristocracy, appeal to the pride of the Hispano-Muslims and fill high offices with men who would owe their power to him alone and not to their ancestry.

His energy and decisiveness made it possible for him very much to be his own chief minister. He also designated his chosen heir, the prince al-Hakam, more than a decade before his death, thereby avoiding dangerous succession rivalries; he delegated responsibilities to his son, thereby giving considerable executive experience to the future caliph. He increased the prestige of the monarch himself by developing further than ever before the court protocol, which duly impressed all provincial governors and foreign ambassadors who were permitted, after properly kissing the floor, to crawl towards the royal dais.

Ultimately the régime rested on naked force. Roughly one-third of the huge state income was devoted to the maintenance of a standing army of 100,000 men. The élite troops of the palace guard were Leonese and Frankish mercenaries, and east European Slavs – men who could be counted upon not to have sentimental ties to the predominantly Hispano-Muslim population of the capital. The bulk of the general soldiery was Berber, and troop units were organized and housed so as to break down residual tribal loyalties.

Neither race nor religion was important in the caliph's personal and arbitrary choice of high military and civil officials. As a way of retaining the religious loyalty of the great majority of his subjects, the caliph ostentatiously used his private income for the upkeep of mosques and the support of municipal charities. It was equally a matter of policy at all times to maintain cordial relations with the Christian and Jewish communities, and to entertain elaborately the embassies of the great Christian powers: Byzantium, the Norse, Frankish and Saxon German empires. Immediately to the north the caliph maintained almost constant good relations with queen Toda of Navarre, and alternately engaged in war and diplomacy with Leon and Castile – giving preference, whenever possible, to diplomacy.

Not the least factor in the great prestige enjoyed by the caliphate among its northern neighbours was the reputation of Islamic medicine. By the early tenth century all the important surviving Greek medical treatises had been translated in Damascus, Baghdad or Cairo, and knowledge of these translations had spread to North Africa and to al-Andalus. The reading of Galen spurred the idea that disease could be cured, but the texts themselves were full of errors and superstitions. Arab physicians (unlike those of Europe before the Renaissance) practised dissection, yet their drawings and anatomical texts simply repeated the errors of the revered Galen, ignoring the results of their own dissections.

Far more important than Galen was the accumulated botanical and pharmacological lore of the entire Orient as codified and practised by physicians of all religions living under Islamic rule. Rhubarb and sodium sulphate, of Chinese origin, were widely used as laxatives, and opium was a well-known narcotic. Tannic acid was used to control diarrhoea and minor intestinal bleeding. It was employed also as an antidote to metallic and alkaline poisons, and was applied to skin ulcers. Tartar emetic and antimony salts were used to treat hookworm; swallowed in small doses, they were supposed to do away with various internal parasites by inducing the patient to vomit. Many other plants, among them cloves, pepper, musk, amber, Chinese ginger, nutmeg, camphor and betel nuts, were prescribed for the relief of all kinds of internal symptoms. There are no records permitting us to judge the efficacy of such treatments, but there may have been a considerable measure of both physical and psychological relief of pain. From both the Greeks and the Indians came an emphasis on personal hygiene and moderate diet, and the plants mentioned above doubtless served to restore a jaded appetite and by so doing to contribute to the natural recovery of the patient whose disease could not be diagnosed.

At the same time the records concerning a handful of distinguished physicians go considerably beyond the practice of hygiene and pharmacology. Rhazes (865–925), a royal physician in Baghdad, was a skilled observer who ridiculed the notion, very popular among his contemporaries, that urinalysis was sufficient to diagnose everything. He is credited with having accurately distinguished smallpox from measles – a more significant accomplishment than the modern reader might suppose, since measles was formerly almost as dread a disease as smallpox. He also popularized, though he may not have invented, the use of animal gut for stitching.

Many of the most famous doctors were surgeons as well. In fact, while the Arabs awarded greater prestige to medical than to surgical procedures, they did not make the immense distinction between them that was characteristic of Europe, where, until the late eighteenth century, barbers doubled as surgeons, to the great detriment of the development of scientific medicine. The Cordoban physician Abulcasis (d. 1013) declared that Arab surgical progress was being held back by the lack of both anatomical and Galenic studies. He performed successful operations for fistula, goitre, gallstones, hernia and enlarged arteries. In treating intestinal injuries, of which there were many among soldiers, he held the edges of the wound together and applied large ants. He also engaged in trepanning, the process of opening the skull to relieve the pressure of tumours, and he recommended cauterization in the treatment of apoplexy and epilepsy as well as in surgery and cases of severe haemorrhage.

There is no way of knowing what measure of success Abulcasis achieved with his trepanning, nor with his startling

uses of ants and of cauterization. Clearly, from the accounts of
the Middle Ages, some exceptional human beings must have
been able to withstand pain that no one has had to bear since
the development of modern anaesthesia. Some of the patients
must have recovered, for otherwise their doctors would have
been completely discredited. There must have been much
intuitive and empirical knowledge involved which is not
reflected in the sparse documents. There is simply not enough
information to account completely for the reputation of
Islamic medicine and surgery. But princes and wealthy men
came from all over western Europe to be treated by Cordoban
physicians in the tenth century, and the work of these physicians
was one of the cultural glories of the caliphate.

45

26, 27 Lid of an ivory casket: the inscription on the casket relates to al-Hakam (left). Marble trough, one of the few remaining objects which reflect the style of al-Mansur's palace, Medinat al-Zahira. The inscription refers to al-Mansur, and is dated 987–88 (right).

Abd-al-Rahman's son and successor, al-Hakam II (961–76), generally continued his father's policies and administrative methods. He was less forceful, more intellectual and religious. He spent lavishly in collecting his library of 400,000 volumes, and made extensive additions to the Great Mosque, as much out of personal piety as of family policy. He is said to have been disturbed by the well-nigh universal flouting of the Koranic prohibitions on alcohol, but to have decided not to try to extirpate the prosperous vineyards of his subjects since they would then have been forced to substitute an inferior liquor made from figs. For his top executive officers al-Hakam depended upon two self-made men: al-Mushafy, who came from a modest Berber family in Valencia, and a leading general named Ghalib, who was a liberated slave.

The death of al-Hakam caused a grave political crisis. He had had only two sons, one of whom had died in early childhood,

and the second of whom, Hisham, was a sickly boy of eleven. Some eight months before his death the caliph, who was already mortally ill, and whose younger brother al-Mugira was acting as regent, had compelled the main palace officials to swear an oath of loyalty to the presumptive heir, prince Hisham. But the succession of a weak pre-adolescent boy would no more go unchallenged in Muslim than in Christian Spain. Palace eunuchs attempted, without his consent, to name al-Mugira as caliph. On orders of the *de facto* chief minister al-Mushafy, the unfortunate young regent was strangled in order to assure the succession of Hisham II (976–1009).

The true prime movers in the accession of Hisham were the boy's mother, a Basque woman named Subh, and his tutor and estate manager, Ibn Abi Amir, who for simplicity's sake we will refer to henceforth by his later, adopted name, of al-Mansur, 'the victorious one'. Since al-Mansur was to be the virtual

47

dictator of Islamic Spain for more than twenty years, it is worth noting the stages of his career. In the year 967, through the direct influence of Subh, he had been named tutor to the royal princes, and then master of the mint. During the following few years he acquired control of the palace police and also acted as quartermaster in Africa during one of General Ghalib's campaigns. In 975 he became inspector-general of the mercenary troops quartered in Cordoba; during his years as mint master he had become wealthy enough to build a personal palace and to make ostentatious gifts to important members of the harem and of the military élite.

At the death of al-Hakam he allied himself with Mushafy and Subh to ensure the succession of his eleven-year-old pupil, Hisham, and he was commanding officer of the detail which strangled the regent al-Mugira. Certainly between 976 and 978, and perhaps both earlier and later, he was Subh's lover as well as the manager of her son's properties and education. In 978 he married the daughter of Ghalib, and by 981 he had become both military and civil master of the state by eliminating Mushafy and Ghalib. He never dared to overthrow Hisham, or was he perhaps fully satisfied with the reality of dictatorial power without having to assume the title of caliph? He courted public opinion by abolishing a few particularly hated taxes, by purging al-Hakam's library, and by carefully staged appearances as a 'fellow worker' in the building of additions to the Great Mosque. Though there were occasional plots against him, often master-minded by Subh, who had slowly come to hate her former protégé and lover, al-Mansur ruled Cordoba from 981 until his death in 1002.

Through his semi-annual *razzias* in the north, al-Mansur has acquired a particularly evil reputation in Christian historiography, and the leading recent historian of Islamic Spain, E. Lévi-Provençal, has described his campaigns under the heading of 'Holy War'. Once again, the evidence is slender, but what is available does not indicate religious fanaticism in either military or personal matters. Christian troops were regularly

48

28 Beatus's Commentary on the Apocalypse of St John, with its vision of the Church's suffering and its promise of ultimate triumph, brought forth many illuminated copies in Mozarabic Spain. Shown here is a leaf from an eleventh-century version. ▶

enrolled in the élite units of the Cordoban army, as much under al-Mansur as under earlier rulers. In 981, when he fought a decisive battle against his father-in-law Ghalib, the latter's army included Castilian troops under count Garci Fernandez, Navarrese troops under a son of king Sancho Garces II, and Leonese troops which had been sent by Ramiro III. Christian soldiers were thus present in both armies, and the specific royal aid to Ghalib by the northern princes was quite obviously motivated by considerations of the 'balance of power': the need to prevent a potentially aggressive dictator from controlling the entire resources of the strongest single state in the peninsula.

In the years between 984 and 987 al-Mansur supplied to Vermudo II of Galicia and Leon the troops which enabled him to hold his throne against rebellious local nobles. In 989 he attacked Castile for the understandable reason that count Garci Fernandez was supporting the rebellion of one of al-Mansur's sons against his father. Through one of his marriages al-Mansur was the son-in-law of Sancho Garces II of Navarre. When the royal grandfather came to Cordoba in 992 to visit his daughter and grandson he was housed and entertained in al-Mansur's personal palace, al-Zahira; scolded for his occasional desertions of the historic Cordoba-Pamplona alliance, he was permitted to kiss the floor when coming into the presence of his son-in-law, and to kiss the hand of his Islamic grandson. In 993 the Cordoban dictator married a Leonese princess, who so far as we know did not convert, and who in any case returned to Leon after his death and became a nun. At the same time, when Cordoban troops sacked the city of Santiago in 997, they used chained Leonese captives to carry back to Cordoba the bells of the cathedral. They also, by order of the dictator, protected the tomb of Santiago, and the monk who was guarding it. In general, the scattered evidence concerning al-Mansur would suggest that he was principally motivated by personal power and by the acquisition of booty for his troops; but a raid on Santiago was a perfect opportunity both to humiliate the Christian north as a whole and to curry favour with fanatical religious elements at home. The urban populace of Cordoba was never as tolerant as their rulers, and would celebrate the appearance of Christian captives bearing the weight of booty which was important both for its material and symbolic value. The capture of Santiago must also have pleased the orthodox Malikite theologians, but they were not nearly so powerful at this time as they had been in the ninth century.

When al-Mansur died in 1002 Islamic military, political and economic power had dominated the peninsula for almost three hundred years. At no time had that dominance been more spectacular than in the second half of the tenth century. But beneath the surface, Cordoba was neither so strong, nor the Christian kings so weak, as the dynastic and military facts of the moment might indicate. After 1002 the caliphate disintegrated rapidly and a new period opened, in which Islamic Spain retained its economic and cultural leadership, but Christian Spain forged a military power and began to develop political and social institutions. This ended decisively whatever chance there may have been, from the eighth to the tenth century, that Spain would become permanently part of the Islamic world.

The rapid disintegration of the caliphate during the decade following the death of al-Mansur altered decisively the political configuration of Spain. In al-Andalus the eleventh century was the era of the so-called *taifa* (party) kingdoms, ruled by Hispano-Muslim, Berber or Slav dynasties. The most important of those bordering on Christian Spain were Saragossa, Toledo and Badajoz. Further south the principal *taifa* states were Seville, Granada, Almeria and Denia. The decline of Cordoba which made possible the rise of the *taifas* facilitated also the political recovery and the expansion of the northern Christian kingdoms. Leadership lay with the kings of Navarre, Sancho the Great (1000–35) and his son Ferdinand I (1035–65), but the principalities of Galicia, Leon, Castile, Aragon and Catalonia jealously maintained their separate identities and their potential claims to primacy within the Christian territories.

Despite decentralization and civil war Islamic Spain maintained the same high level of economic activity as in the tenth century. Conceivably the decline of Cordoba, the central land power, may have contributed to the increased commercial and piratical prosperity of Seville, Almeria and Denia. In any case the combined wealth and military weakness of the *taifa* kingdoms presented a unique opportunity to the crude, but increasingly populous and militarily skilful Christian states. Following the example of Sancho the Great they developed a tributary system whereby the Islamic states paid specific annual quantities of gold in order to enjoy the military 'protection' of their northern neighbours.

By the middle of the century the Christian princes had negotiated territorial deals with each other, whereby, for example, Saragossa paid its tribute to Castile, Toledo its to

29   Ferdinand I of Castile and Navarre and queen Sancha are presented with a Prayer Book (*Libro de Horas*) by Petrus, its scribe.

Leon, and Badajoz and Seville sent theirs to Galicia. This *paria* (tribute) system flooded the north with gold as early as the 1020s, and made Christian Spain one of the three European centres of financial prosperity, the other two being northern Italy and Flanders. But whereas in the latter areas manufactures and commerce were responsible for the flow of gold, in Spain the acquisition of precious metal resulted almost solely from the levying of tribute on the industrious south. Christian knights bought weapons, armour, equipment for their heavy cavalry and luxury goods. Monasteries bought land, and the services of Muslim artisans and builders. In this century Christian Spain developed several of its characteristic traditions which were to affect not only the entire *Reconquista* but the later style of imperial development in America: the preference for investment in land rather than commerce and industry; the notion that manual labour was proper for Muslims, Jews or Indians, but that the function of Christian Spaniards was to rule; the idea of gaining wealth by levying tribute based upon superior military power.

30   The *taifa* kingdoms at the fall of the caliphate of Cordoba (1031).

31 Santiago. Detail from the Portico de la Gloria, depicting six of the twenty-four elders of the tribes of Israel.

Expansion and prosperity were accompanied by european-ization. From the eighth to the tenth century the tiny Christian kingdoms had been either physically isolated from Europe or too preoccupied with the power of Cordoba to pay much attention to Europe. Tenth-century Spanish chronicles make frequent mention of Cordoba, but none of Carolingian or Capetian France. The focal points of Spanish Christian con-sciousness were Toledo and Santiago, not Rome. All this changed radically during the eleventh century. Sancho the Great established regular contact with the Roman curia and preached the adoption of the Benedictine rule in the monasteries of Navarre and the western kingdoms, where Visigothic traditions had predominated. The Catalans, whose religious life had been dominated by the archbishopric of Narbonne since the time of Charlemagne, now sent regular embassies to Rome. It was in Catalonia also that the first Cluniac monasteries were founded, and by the deliberate decision of Sancho they were invited to establish themselves in Navarre and Castile. A key feature of the Cluniac reform, from the moment of its origin in tenth-century France, had been the direct dependence

55

of the monasteries on Rome rather than on the local feudal lords. In northern Spain their arrival strengthened both clerical and royal communications with Rome, introduced French methods of agriculture and forestry, encouraged the Benedictine rule with its emphasis on manual labour, and made the Spanish clergy conscious of the differences which had developed quietly over the centuries between the Visigothic and the Roman forms of church service.

Under Ferdinand I and under Alfonso VI (1065–1109) Castile, rather than Navarre or Leon, became the principal dynastic holding, and both sovereigns continued the europeanizing policies of Sancho the Great. The first peninsular crusade was preached against Barbastro, under the auspices of pope Alexander II, in 1064. His successor, Gregory VII (who had also struggled with the German emperor, Henry IV, over the investiture of bishops), insisted on the adoption throughout Spain of the Roman rite. He was assisted in this effort by Alfonso's Burgundian wife Constance. The king himself, while he prized good relations with Rome, and had in 1077 doubled

32 Ferdinand I of Castile: a stylized portrait from a twelfth-century illuminated manuscript.

33   An example of Visigothic script from the end of the ninth century: extract from Smaragdus's *On the Rule of St Benedict*.

his annual subsidies to the order of Cluny, nevertheless pleaded for delay on behalf of his many Castilian and Leonese subjects who were attached to the Visigothic tradition.

When in the course of the 1080s the Roman rite was imposed in all Alfonso's lands, central and western Spain lost touch with the Old Testament, considerable portions of which had been read in the Visigothic mass, and also with the Visigothic script, in which the Isidoran cultural heritage had been handed down from generation to generation over some four hundred years. Alfonso VI also chartered the great Cluniac monasteries of Sahagun (1079) and San Juan de la Peña (1090). By the end of his reign the entire church hierarchy was French, and most of the bishops were products of Cluniac training. The sovereign encouraged the monasteries to establish colonies of bourgeois in their environs; he also permitted the granting of charters which exempted these bourgeois from royal taxes and facilitated the naturalization of French and Italian immigrants. We have little specific information about the population of new towns, but we do know, for example, that Jaca, founded in 1077, had a population of about two thousand in the year 1137, 78 per cent of whom were listed as being of French origin.

Alfonso balanced europeanization with renewed attention to the tradition of Santiago: the conviction that the mortal remains of St James the Greater, one of the twelve apostles, had been miraculously transported from the Holy Land to the remote Galician town where they were discovered early in the ninth century. Between 1075 and 1095 (the latter being the year in which Urban II announced the first crusade to the Holy Land) large-scale bridge and road improvements were made along the route to Compostela. Colonies of French merchants were established at short intervals to serve the needs of pilgrims reaching Pamplona from Toulouse or Narbonne, and then crossing northern Spain via Logroño, Burgos, Carrion de los Condes, Leon and Lugo.

Meanwhile, Islamic Spain, although politically fragmented, managed both to pay enormous sums of gold to its Christian 'protectors' and to maintain an economy far superior to that of the northern kingdoms. Skilled artisans, many of them Mozarabs, produced metalwork, jewellery, glass, armaments and textiles which were prized throughout northern Spain and France. The best horses, hunting-dogs and falcons were also bred and trained in al-Andalus. The roads were unsafe, but the inns and public baths supplied forms of comfort, cuisine and sensual experience unknown in the north. There was no system of public education, but the bourgeoisie and the civil servants enjoyed a bilingual culture: religion, philosophy, science and diplomatic relations with the East were conducted in Arabic; the vernacular was used in family life, daily housekeeping and local commerce; and poetry employed the resources of both languages.

According to the accounts of Muslim travellers from the East, the people of al-Andalus enjoyed a higher standard of living than those of North Africa or the Arabian peninsula; every man had his own donkey, women wore the veil less and were generally freer in their comportment, and there was greater toleration granted to the sizable Christian and Jewish communities.

Under the caliphate the Arab aristocracy had remained politically powerful, although increasingly challenged by Berber, Slav and native Andalusian families. The break-up of the Cordoban régime and the rise of the *taifa* kingdoms was in large measure an anti-Arab revolution. None of the new dynasties was Arab, and the eleventh century witnessed a general reaction against eastern influences in scholarship and philosophy. There was an extraordinary cultural flowering, comparable in many ways with that of Germany in the nineteenth century. Just as the combination of numerous small sovereignties, economic prosperity, royal patronage of the arts and a patriotic reaction against the French Enlightenment had stimulated the cultural development of Germany, so the political and cultural rivalries of the many *taifas*, and the reaction against imported Middle Eastern culture, stimulated the native culture of al-Andalus. Princes bid against one another for the services of the finest minstrels, poets, diplomats and chroniclers. One of the main forms of poetry was the panegyric addressed to the prince and celebrating his wisdom, his magnanimity, his prowess, his perspicacity in the choice of poets – and, of course, his generosity in rewarding their verses.

The commonest theme of poetry was love in all its varieties: heterosexual and homosexual, sensual and platonic, sophisticated and naïve, fulfilled and frustrated. Extreme refinement of language and imagery, with little spontaneous feeling (a species of euphuistic tradition), characterized the poetry composed in classical Arabic. Earthier images, rhythms and emotions were expressed in Romance. It is difficult, and inevitably dangerous, to generalize about a style of life on the basis of belles-lettres. From the reading of eleventh-century Hispano-Arab poetry, however, one cannot help sensing among the literate ruling class a widespread boredom and cynicism, an appetite for novel sexual sensations, and a striving after verbal cleverness for its own sake. The beauty of gardens is also frequently celebrated, with emphasis placed upon the landscape as remodelled by man, rather than upon the pristine beauty of nature.

We know very little about the attitude of eleventh-century Christians towards the sophisticated literary culture and social life of the *taifa* aristocracies. But clearly the Christian rulers were tempted by their own military superiority, and by the increasing pressure of their farmers, herdsmen and crusading clergymen, to expand southward, and ultimately to substitute direct conquest for the tributary system. The issues and the problems involved may be illustrated by the careers of the two leading personalities concerning whom we have some detailed knowledge: king Alfonso VI, and his still more famous vassal, Rodrigo Diaz de Vivar, the Cid (from the Arabic title *Sidi*, or Lord).

Alfonso was the second son of Ferdinand I. As such he had inherited Leon in 1065, while Castile, now considered to be the most important dynastic holding, had gone to his elder brother Sancho. As had happened before, and was to happen repeatedly in the ensuing centuries, the royal brothers almost immediately began to fight one another for the entire heritage. Between 1065 and 1072 Alfonso was twice defeated by Castilian armies whose field commander was the Cid. Alfonso had lived as a political refugee in both Badajoz and Toledo, and had continued,

34 Opposite, wooden chest thought to have belonged to the Cid.

35 Left, Alfonso VI, as portrayed in a twelfth-century illuminated manuscript.

36 Below, marble relief of the mid-eleventh century pictures a warrior conquering a city.

in league with his sister Urraca, to plot against his brother. When the latter was mysteriously murdered in 1072, Alfonso claimed the throne of Castile, but was recognized as the legitimate sovereign only after taking an oath, administered by the Cid, to the effect that he had had nothing to do with the death of king Sancho.

Having united the realms of Castile and Leon, and easily dominating the third brother who reigned in Galicia, Alfonso turned his attention to the *taifa* of Toledo. Several factors made Toledo a logical objective for Christian territorial expansion. It had a large Mozarabic population and a long tradition of revolt against the emirs and caliphs of Cordoba. It dominated the valley of the Tagus river, and migrating Christian herdsmen during the century had gradually but steadily colonized the steppe lands between the tenth-century Duero frontier and the Tagus. There were two fairly equal factions within the city, one patronized by the *taifa* king of Badajoz, the other by Alfonso. Between 1080 and 1085 the latter complained of the debased coinage in which the tribute was being paid; making himself spokesman for the real or imagined grievances of the Mozarabic community of Toledo, he laid intermittent siege to the city, and conducted military forays deep into Andalusia.

In 1085 Alfonso entered the city, offering generous terms of self-government to the Muslim and Mozarabic communities, guaranteeing for a transitional period the locally beloved Visigothic rite, and referring to himself as the 'Emperor of the Two Religions'. At the same time, however, he boasted of his unconquerable armies, spoke scornfully of the *taifa* princes generally, and demanded either increased tribute or direct rule of Saragossa, Seville and Granada. The threatened princes felt unable militarily to contain Alfonso. They had to consider which would be the lesser of two evils: direct rule by Alfonso, or an appeal to African military power as an alternative to Christian rule.

North Africa had recently been unified by a pious, puritanical Berber dynasty, the Almoravids. These were fanatical Muslims

37 A stylized view of Toledo, from the tenth-century *Codex Aemilianensis*. On the battlements are the chief citizens, the royal family and the clergy.

with almost no knowledge of either Middle Eastern or Hispanic culture. They were looked upon with considerable favour, however, by the Malikite theologians who were still politically powerful in Andalusia, but whose spiritual authority had been greatly undermined by the quasi-pagan culture of the *taifas*. Fear of Alfonso, the pleas of the Malikite leaders and the absence of any military alternative forced the *taifa* kings, under the leadership of al-Mutamid of Seville, to send an embassy to the austere Almoravid chieftain Yusuf. The latter was in no hurry to save his effete brethren, in whose manner towards him he clearly sensed an element of personal scorn. But the next year, 1086, he brought over an experienced and swift-moving army

63

whose march through Andalusia obliged Alfonso to lift the siege of Saragossa and hurry to defend his southern frontier. In a see-saw battle near Badajoz the Almoravid cavalry suddenly routed the Christian army with a flanking attack, and king Alfonso barely escaped with his life.

Nevertheless, there was nothing decisive, either politically or militarily, about this first encounter. Yusuf returned to Africa, and Alfonso continued to conduct plunder raids and threaten the *taifa* kings with annexation. Though it is impossible to reconstruct his calculations in detail, Alfonso must have counted upon the Cid to reinforce his own military strength. Relations between the two had varied greatly over the years. The Cid had been the field commander of the Castilian armies under Sancho, and had administered the oath which had made possible the accession of Alfonso in 1072. He had performed several diplomatic services for Alfonso, and the latter, seeking a firm conciliation with his formidable vassal, had offered in marriage his niece Jimena.

In 1081 the Cid had conducted an unauthorized raid on Toledo, for which he had been exiled, and for the next five years his relationship to Alfonso was, to say the least, ambiguous. He swore an oath never to bear arms against his king, yet took service with the king of Saragossa, whose state was a tributary of Castile, and whose territories were coveted by the several Aragonese and Catalan principalities. At the head of Saragossan armies he inflicted defeats upon the Christian king of Aragon as well as on the rival Muslim states of Lerida and Valencia. He appears also to have offered to conquer Valencia on behalf of Saragossa. He played no role in the Castilian occupation of Toledo, remaining inactive both when Alfonso briefly besieged Saragossa and when the Castilian monarch hurried south to meet the invading Almoravids. From the epic poem which bears his name, and from scattered references to him in Muslim chronicles, it is clear that the Cid had no compunctions about serving Muslim rulers. He was, literally, making his living according to the financial rewards and the cultural styles available to him in prosperous eastern Spain. The only limitation which he placed upon his opportunism was the avoidance of a direct clash with the king of Castile.

After his sobering defeat at Badajoz, Alfonso sought reconciliation with the Cid. In addition, his puppet ruler at Toledo, Alcadir, found himself unable to control the city, and Alfonso transferred him to the conveniently vacant *taifa* throne of Valencia. Apparently he offered the Cid the role of protector and tribute-collector in this wealthy kingdom, in whose affairs the Cid had already intervened while employed by Saragossa. However, the Cid did not aid Alfonso in his renewed struggle against the Almoravids, and Alcadir, counting on the arrival of the Almoravids, withheld his tribute payments from the Cid.

In these circumstances, the Cid decided, in about 1090, to conquer Valencia for himself. Christian Barcelona and Muslim Lerida, in alliance with Alcadir, appealed to Alfonso VI for help against the latter's ambitious vassal-in-exile. Just as the Cid had always stopped short of open hostility towards Alfonso, so the latter refused military aid to the Cid's enemies. By 1094 the Cid was able both to defeat Barcelona and Lerida, and to take Valencia itself from the Almoravids. Much as Alfonso had done at Toledo in 1085, the Cid offered generous terms to the conquered city: the maintenance of the existing municipal government, protection of the property of those not opposed to his régime, religious toleration, no increase in taxation, and the use of Mozarabic rather than Castilian troops to occupy the city. However, the need to reward his army after four years of difficult fighting led him very soon to confiscate both agricultural and urban property. And in his irritation with continued plots against his rule, he evicted the Muslim population from the inner city and replaced them with Christians. He did not hesitate to torture and burn any wealthy Muslims whom he could accuse of treason. Though probably indifferent himself in matters of religion, he appointed a crusading Cluniac bishop for whom toleration was a vice, not a virtue. In this manner he was able to rule Valencia until his death in 1099.

65

The careers of Alfonso VI and of the Cid illustrate a number of important general characteristics of the eleventh century. Christian Spain was expanding both demographically and militarily. Its chieftains were confident of their new strength, and ambitious to acquire wealth and to exercise power. Wealth was available to them first in the form of tribute payments, and then in the form of direct conquest. Although Alfonso VI encouraged the immigration of French bourgeois, he and all the other Christian rulers of the century thought far more in terms of exploiting the Muslim economy than of developing a more sophisticated economy in their northern lands. Their attitude towards Muslim refinement was mixed. They enjoyed the high quality of manufactures and luxury goods, and the services of Muslim artisans; they practised concubinage, though probably not to the same extent as did the *taifa* aristocracy; and they proudly defended their rude masculine virtues against a literary culture which they were unable to appreciate.

Under the pressure of Rome, and of their own leading churchmen, they preached the crusade in connection with their territorial forays and pressed for the adoption of the Roman rite. But in the interest of political unity within their own dominions they granted exceptions and delays in the process of romanization. In order to counter the psychological aggressiveness of the popes they improved, and greatly publicized, the pilgrimage route to Santiago. Meanwhile, the *taifa* kingdoms, wealthy, tolerant and militarily weak, were caught between the increasing aggressiveness of the Christian kings and the rising power of the primitive, fanatical Almoravids. Due perhaps as much to the political errors of Alfonso VI as to the actual depredations of Christian armies, they called in North Africa to redress the balance in Spain.

The appeal to the Almoravids was a blunt confession of weakness, and was understood as such by Yusuf. Quick to judge the impotence of the *taifa* kings, while somewhat awed by their worldliness, he was slow to intervene in al-Andalus. Brusque, uneducated and speaking little Arabic, he appealed to the

Muslim lower classes through his simple dignity, religious austerity and anti-intellectualism. Though apparently direct in manner, he was perfectly capable of following a courteous reception by torture and murder. He had able generals who were his loyal subordinates, and he was well thought of by the orthodox Malikite theologians. He looked upon the Christians as infidels and felt that their *taifa* victims had deserved what they got. Thus the Almoravid invasion, while it put a temporary end to Christian expansion, was also a psychological and cultural defeat for Spanish Islam. The combination of official crusade propaganda from the north with Almoravid fanaticism in the south injected a greater degree of religious animosity into the fighting at the turn of the twelfth century than had been present during the decades after the fall of the caliphate.

During the ensuing century, generally speaking, neither Muslim nor Christian rulers were able to consolidate the resources potentially available to them. The Almoravids needed some fifteen years to establish their sovereignty throughout the *taifa* area. Terrorism against the urban populace and assassination of key opponents were necessary to subdue Granada, and Seville was sacked in 1091. Murcia, Denia, Badajoz and Valencia had to be subdued successively, and the local élites sabotaged Almoravid authority as much as they could. The conquerors enjoyed a fair degree of popular support by lowering taxes, establishing relative 'law and order' following the extreme instability of the preceding century, and by their tough treatment of the Jews and Mozarabs, a large proportion of whom migrated north during the Almoravid era.

Like many earlier groups of primitive tribesmen, the Almoravids rapidly succumbed to the sophisticated civilization which they had conquered. Their rule was under challenge in Morocco during the 1120s, and they had been swept from power in both North Africa and Spain by 1147. The new conquerors, who managed for a half-century to unite the Islamic world from Egypt to Andalusia, were the Almohads, an orthodox, fanatically monotheist tribe originating in the Atlas

38 The horseshoe arch, here incorporated in one of the city-gates of Toledo.

39, 40, 41 Tiles (below) and a complicated textile design (opposite), characteristic products of the elaborate skill of the craftsmen of Islamic Spain.

mountains. Primitive physical vigour was their chief advantage in fighting the Almoravids, but they claimed also to be conducting a holy war against the descendants of Yusuf, whom they accused of a quasi-Christian heresy, to the effect that the attributes of God were incompatible with the simplicity of the divine essence.

Culturally, the Almohad victory was important in that they recognized the spiritual supremacy of Baghdad, and imported to Spain the Middle Eastern philosophy and science which had been largely boycotted during nearly two centuries of the caliphate and the *taifas*. The most original portions of Hispano-Muslim culture had been poetic and artistic. The *zejel*, the horseshoe arch (of Visigothic origin, but greatly developed and varied by Muslim architects), the decoration of textiles and tiles, all showed artistic qualities unique to al-Andalus. The independent claims of the Umayyads, both as emirs (756–929) and as caliphs (929–c. 1010), and then the flourishing of the *taifas* (c. 1010–90), had consciously encouraged such originality. At the same time Malikite orthodoxy, and political-geographical isolation from the centres of the Islamic world, had reduced the influence of eastern philosophy and science.

In the cosmopolitan cities of Baghdad, Damascus and Cairo the most original cultural developments took place in the fields of botany, astronomy, mathematics and grammar. Newly created fruits, dyes, types of cereal and rice plants had always been freely adopted in al-Andalus. Particular mathematical and grammatical treatises had also been known to a few scholars in tenth-century Cordoba. But wide interest in Persian philosophy and art, in Greek philosophy and medicine, and wide knowledge of algebra and quadratic surds, large-scale translation and comparative philological study of Persian, Greek and Arab literature were much more marked in the twelfth century under Almohad auspices than they had been since the time of Abd-al-Rahman II (822–52). In part this was a matter of improved communications, in part of the attitude of the rulers, for whom Egypt, Tunis and Morocco were more important subdivisions of the Islamic world than was Andalusia.

By the same token, however, the culture of Islamic Spain in the twelfth century was much less original than that of the previous three centuries. General histories of the Middle Ages never fail to name the two great twelfth-century Cordobans: Averroes (1126–98), and Maimonides (1135–1204). The former was physician to the Almohad caliph Abu Yakub I, and a major Muslim commentator on Aristotle. He was twice exiled from Cordoba, and both his medical methods and his philosophy were completely derived from rather unoriginal Middle Eastern traditions. Maimonides, though born in Cordoba, had experienced the anti-semitism of the Almohad era, and chose to spend his entire adult life in Egypt. As a physician he continued the completely non-experimental reverence for Galen while giving good common-sense advice about moderation in diet, exercise and sexual life. The Almohads were great builders and art patrons, as evidenced by the rapid construction of the port of Gibraltar in the 1160s, the creation of the Giralda in Seville and of the grand mosque in Marrakesh. But during the twelfth century Islamic Spain was only a cultural appendage of eastern Islam.

42 Title and contents page
from a fifteenth-century
nish copy of *Mishneh Torah*
by Moses Maimonides.

   In the Christian north the twelfth century was characterized
generally by political disunity and the triumph of ranching and
clerical, as against bourgeois, economic interests. Alfonso VI
had been married five times, but his only male heir, born to the
princess Zaida, daughter of king Mutamid of Seville, died in
battle against the Almoravids in 1108. The aging king had two
daughters by two different French wives. One, Urraca, had
married Raymond of Burgundy, and their son eventually
reigned as Alfonso VII (1126–57). The younger, Teresa, had
married Henry of Burgundy, and their son, Afonso Henriques,
was to become the founder of independent Portugal.

71

43　Eleventh-century jewelled chalice belonging to Urraca.

Raymond of Burgundy had also died before his father-in-law, and in a last-minute effort to unite the realms of Castile and Aragon, Alfonso VI of Castile and Leon had married his widowed daughter Urraca to Alfonso I, 'The Battler', king of Aragon (1102–34). Their marriage in 1109, followed shortly by the death of the old king, coincided with a widespread revolt among the peasants and the bourgeois of Aragon. The former demanded a lightening of services due to their landlords. The latter refused to pay a supplementary Easter tax and demanded royal, as against monastic, control of the forests, vineyards and grain-mills. The rural clergy also protested against the economic privileges of the Cluniac monasteries. The revolt spread into Castilian-Leonese territory via the pilgrimage route to Santiago. In both kingdoms the forces of the nobility and the clergy coalesced round Urraca, and the peasants and bourgeois looked to Alfonso. The nobles obtained a pontifical annulment of the marriage (Urraca and Alfonso were second cousins) and in the years 1116 and 1117 several papal bulls required the bourgeois to restore all land and goods which they had confiscated from the monasteries during the previous five years. There is no way of measuring precisely the economic harm which resulted from the defeat of the townsmen, but the general outcome of the struggle between 1109 and 1117 was the triumph of the church and its landlord allies over the peasants and the merchants, many of whom were recent French immigrants.

Throughout the twelfth century the nobles and the clergy of Castile and Leon steadily developed their sheep-raising and wool-exporting activities. The Cantabrican port towns were repopulated in order to handle the wool trade, and Castilian wool competed profitably in the English home market and penetrated Flemish markets to a lesser degree. In Navarre and the Rioja district vineyards and cereals flourished in a country-side of temperate climate and great natural beauty. As the Aragonese gradually extended their sway in the Ebro valley they acquired richly irrigated lands, whose Muslim farmers they encouraged to remain as well-treated tenants of the new Christian ruling class. On the east and west coasts of the penin-sula, Barcelona, Tortosa and Lisbon developed rapidly as commercial centres, encouraged by the decline of Muslim naval power, and by the steady economic and demographic develop-ment of southern France and northern Spain. These economic trends during the twelfth century produced long-term con-sequences in Hispanic history: the anti-bourgeois orientation of Castile; the generally greater tolerance of subject Muslims, the

Mudejars, by the crown of Aragon; and the bourgeois and commercial orientation of Portugal and Catalonia.

European, and particularly French, influences remained strong throughout the century. An important school of translators was created in Toledo under the patronage of the Cluniac archbishop Raymond (1124–51). The translations generally took place in two stages: from Arabic to Romance, and from Romance to Latin. This double process increased the risk of error, especially in cases where the Arabic was already based upon a Greek original. But it was through Toledo that Christian Europe acquired its first imperfect knowledge of Arabic treatises on philosophy, grammar, astronomy and medicine. The quality and energy of Cluniac leadership declined sharply, but their latinizing, romanizing and crusading spirit was taken up by another highly disciplined French order, the Cistercians.

Like the order of Cluny, the Cistercians practised the Benedictine rule and supported the authority of the Roman hierarchy against the tendency of princes to make the local church a kind of family possession. Unlike Cluny, the Cistercian organization gave substantial autonomy to the abbot in charge of each house. The Cistercians chose rural sites, methodically and skilfully clearing forests and draining swamps. Their skills in land reclamation made them especially valuable in conditions of demographic growth and territorial expansion. A whole series of monasteries in Galicia, western Castile and Portugal testify to the extension of the civilized, agricultural frontier of Christian Spain in the twelfth century. Their monasteries were larger and more complex than those of the previous century. Besides containing the usual church and refectory, they were notable for the addition of separate cloisters, workshops and dormitories affording personal privacy to the monks. St Bernard, the founder of the order, had had a taste for natural beauty, for poetic, interior contemplation as well as for austere labour. Whether or not it is reasonable to attribute to his personal influence the choice of sites, the fact is that the Cister-

44   Spain at the death of Alfonso VII (1157).

cians built their houses in locations of great natural beauty,
amidst water and trees, and with their dormitories oriented to
take advantage of the beautiful landscape. In this characteristic
they showed the same aesthetic sensitivity to landscape as did
the builders of the Arab villas in Andalusia.

While rural monasteries were reclaiming land and christian-
izing the relatively primitive western territories, the Almohads
were threatening to roll back the new frontiers which had been
established in the time of Alfonso VI. In line with the crusading
interests of the order, and to meet this specific military threat,
the Cistercian abbot of Fitero in 1158 declared a crusade to
recover Calatrava, and his initiative led to the formation,
between 1160 and 1180, of three monastic societies of knights
pledged to defend the frontiers against Islam: the orders of
Calatrava, Alcantara and Santiago. For almost one hundred
years, until the completion of the thirteenth-century reconquest,

75

45   Knight of the order of St John:
effigy of Bernat de Foixa,
in the family chapel
of the Castell de Foixa.

they defended the southern steppe-land borders of Castile, Extremadura and Portugal. During this time they also became wealthy landlords and cattle-ranchers.

In the middle of the twelfth century Christian Spain formed the three political units which were to persist into modern times: Portugal, Castile and Aragon-Catalonia. Alfonso VI had married his illegitimate younger daughter Teresa to Henry of Burgundy, and had awarded him the county of Portugal. Their son Afonso Henriques had steadily resisted the efforts of his cousin Alfonso VII to claim sovereignty over Portugal. In 1139 he had proclaimed himself king, had appealed for papal protection as a 'vassal' of the Holy See, and had been aided in his diplomacy by the Cistercians. Thereafter Portugal was virtually independent, and became officially so with recognition by pope Alexander III in 1179.

In the case of Aragon, a dynastic crisis had been opened by the death of Alfonso I, 'the Battler', in 1134. The late king, deeply religious, had died without an heir, and had willed his dominions to the orders of St John and the Templars. But the Almohads were threatening to reconquer the entire Ebro valley, and Alfonso VII of Castile was ready to claim the kingdom as his. In these circumstances the Aragonese nobility urged 'the Battler's' younger brother, the monk Ramiro, to mount the throne. Ramiro returned to the secular world, married, and then affianced his infant daughter, Petronilla, to count Ramon Berenguer IV of Barcelona. In this manner the hill kingdom of Aragon was dynastically joined to the commercial and agricultural county of Barcelona to create the kingdom of Aragon-Catalonia.

But neither the energy of Afonso Henriques, nor the marital good fortune of the ex-monk Ramiro, nor the political errors of Alfonso VII of Castile, serve to explain the tripartite division of the peninsula. None of the earlier political units of Christian Spain had had natural or linguistic frontiers. Galicia and Portugal formed a linguistic unit, but a political frontier was drawn at the river Minho in about 1140, and has existed ever since. Leon might be distinguished from Castile in that its sovereignty was established earlier, and in the degree of Mozarabic cultural influence, but there is no natural or clear cultural border between them. Navarre and Aragon were small hill kingdoms straddling both slopes of the Pyrenees, with frontiers and populations varying according to the strengths of individual rulers, and the vicissitudes of war in southern France and northern Spain. Catalonia was the most distinct of the units, with its own language and its long political and cultural connections with France. But its frontiers also shifted frequently, and between the ninth and the twelfth centuries, neither on the French side nor along the Mediterranean, were those frontiers truly linguistic or geographical. Neither the physical map of the Hispanic peninsula, nor the detailed political history of the early Middle Ages will reveal logical reasons for the eventual emergence of Portugal, Castile and Aragon-Catalonia as the major sovereignties. Nor must it be forgotten that Navarre continued until 1512 as a frequently independent unit, and that Leon was again separated from Castile between 1158 and 1230.

46   Polygonal exterior of the Templars' church of Vera Cruz, Segovia.

But for the purposes of the reconquest, now being consciously pursued, the three kingdoms agreed in advance on the jurisdictions of each. The successive treaties of Tudilen (1151), Cazorla (1179) and Almizra (1244) delineated clearly the respective spheres of Castile and Aragon: Andalusia and most of Murcia to Castile; Valencia, the Balearics and Alicante to Aragon. There were similar understandings between Portugal and Castile assigning the Algarve to Portugal. Nothing illustrates better than these treaties the supreme confidence, the long-range planning capacity, the imperial psychology and the combination of crusading and tribute-collecting traditions of Christian Spain in the High Middle Ages. Their inability to unify their own dominions retarded, but never placed in real doubt, the eventual triumph of Christian Spain and Portugal over the still prosperous and populous provinces ruled by the Almohads.

78

47   Miniature from the Book of the order of Santiago, showing knights of the order.

III THIRTEENTH-CENTURY
CONQUEST AND SYNTHESIS

Not until the last years of the long reign of Alfonso VIII of Castile (1158–1214) were Christian armies able to win a major victory over the Muslims. The renewed rivalry between Leon and Castile (the two realms had different kings again from 1158 to 1230) effectively prevented the Castilian king from mobilizing the full military potential of the north, and after his stunning defeat by the Almohads at Alarcos in 1195, his fellow Christian sovereigns formed temporary diplomatic alliances against him. But in the year 1212 a great Christian army, with French contingents as well as representatives of all the peninsular kingdoms, joined in a crusade patronized by pope Innocent III. At the battle of Las Navas de Tolosa, at one of the crucial passes leading from the *meseta* of New Castile to the valley of the Guadalquivir, the Christians literally destroyed the Almohad army. Because of severe droughts in the ensuing few years, and perhaps in part also because of the stench and disease caused by thousands of unburied corpses, the Christians did not proceed to an immediate occupation of the captured towns; but when Alfonso VIII died in 1214 the path was clearly open for a full Christian conquest of al-Andalus.

Historians have long debated whether the spectacular Christian advances of the thirteenth century should be labelled 'conquest' or 'reconquest'. In that al-Andalus was a densely populated, urban and heavily orientalized civilization, it bore very little resemblance to the Visigothic Andalusia which Arab-led armies had occupied in 711. In this sense, certainly, the Christians 'conquered' al-Andalus. Furthermore, with the exception of the second half of the eleventh century, during the reigns of Ferdinand I and Alfonso VI, at no time before the thirteenth century could Christian rulers have conceived any

48 Central panel of an altarpiece, attributed to Andres Marzal de Sax (*fl.* 1400), which depicts James I of Aragon-Catalonia killing a Moorish king with the help of St George – a reference to James's victory at Puig de Cebolla in 1237.

practical prospect of ruling the entire peninsula. But medieval chronicles did preserve the memory of Roman and Visigothic rule, the majority of the Andalusian population did speak a Romance dialect, and the church had worked steadily and successfully to inculcate in the population of the northern kingdoms the idea that the peninsula as a whole should be reclaimed for Christendom. Historic consciousness in the thirteenth century, and the ethnic-linguistic situation, do justify describing the Christian advance as a 'reconquest'.

The major figures of the thirteenth-century conquest were Ferdinand III of Castile (1217–52) and of Leon after 1230; and James I of Aragon-Catalonia (1213–76). Both sovereigns attained their thrones after troubled minorities. Both were immensely capable and energetic men, single-minded in pursuing the *Reconquista* (in the psychological sense defined above), able to inspire confidence in their leadership, and able to cooperate with each other in dividing 'spheres of influence' between their respective kingdoms. The armies of Aragon-Catalonia contributed somewhat less than did those of Castile, for two principal reasons: Catalan involvement in southern France, where, in fact, Peter II of Aragon died in 1213 defending the cause of the Albigensians at the battle of Muret; and the investment of much Catalan energy in commercial and naval enterprises in the Mediterranean.

The disaster of Las Navas de Tolosa led rapidly to political revolution within al-Andalus. The native Hispano-Muslims had always resented rule by Africans. The only justification of that rule for more than a century had been the inability of local Muslim forces to contain the advancing Christians. Once the Almohads were no longer able to defend Andalusia against the northern invaders there was no reason to tolerate Almohad rule. In the 1220s a leader named Ibn Hud, scion of an important Hispano-Muslim family from Saragossa, overthrew one after another of the Almohad provincial governors. Not strong enough, however, to establish a fully independent régime of his own, he became the tributary of Ferdinand III in much the same fashion as *taifa* kings of the eleventh century had been tributaries of Alfonso VI. In a series of treaties between 1224 and 1236 Ferdinand was able to collect large sums of money, and also to arrange for the peaceful occupation of a number of Andalusian towns by Christian settlers.

The triumph of Ibn Hud took place at about the same time as the attainment of full power in Leon by Ferdinand III, who had inherited that throne from his estranged father in 1230, and had required a few years thereafter to pacify his new dominion. Ferdinand, who was destined to be sainted, possessed a full measure of the crusade psychology. He is referred to in the chronicles as having hanged and boiled many heretics, and once he had achieved full power in both Castile and Leon he was ambitious to forward the full conquest of Andalusia. His demand for the city of Cordoba was more than Ibn Hud could agree to.

49 Ferdinand III, portrayed by a fifteenth-century sculptor as a holy knight on horseback.

50 James I, as he appears on a contemporary seal.

Ferdinand thereupon successfully besieged the ancient capital of the caliphate in 1236. Ibn Hud was overthrown by his partisans for failing to defend the city, and no other Muslim leader was able to create a united resistance.

Logistic and population problems, rather than military obstacles, determined the further tempo of Christian conquest. Jaen fell to Ferdinand in 1246 as part of a deal whereby a Muslim protégé of the Castilian king became the ruler of Granada. The last great city, Seville, was conquered in 1248 after a difficult siege, which included the use of naval contingents brought round Portugal from the Cantabrican coast to blockade the mouth of the Guadalquivir and cut off all supplies from Africa. Meanwhile, a Catalan naval expedition in 1229 had taken Majorca, an Aragonese army had reduced Valencia by siege in 1238, and in that same year the Portuguese, by prior agreement with Castile, had taken Tavira and completed the conquest of

51 Detail of the altarpiece of St George, attributed to the fifteenth-century painter Pedro Nisart, represents the intervention of St George on behalf of James I in his battle against the Moors.

52, 53, 54 Wall paintings of the late thirteenth or early fourteenth century showing (above) James I and his troops entering Valencia, and (below) Catalan knights and archers.

55   The thirteenth-century Reconquest.

the Algarve. This meant that after 1248 only Granada remained under Muslim rule. This arrangement suited the crown of Castile because Granada paid large tribute to Castile and was available as a kind of refuge for Muslim populations expelled from their old homes in other parts of the former Almohad domains.

The swift military occupation of Andalusia in a period of only thirty years posed formidable political and economic problems for the conquerors. They were taking over a heavily populated territory with a highly sophisticated economy, both urban and rural. They brought with them neither the craft skills, in metal work, leather goods, textiles, etc., nor the knowledge of plants and irrigation systems necessary to maintain that economy. Their soldiers expected to be handsomely rewarded for their military feats, and many thought of themselves as permanent emigrants from the harsh climate of the Castilian *meseta*. In the first years of the conquest, the prosperous Muslim farms were turned over to Christian owners who hoped to live off the profits, without having to displace the working population. The cities, however, were almost immediately emptied of their Muslim inhabitants, in part as a measure of military security, in part to provide soldiers with wealth in the form of real estate. The displacement of the Muslim craftsmen and merchants led to a catastrophic decline in the entire urban economy of southern Spain. It created immediate disaffection in the form of political refugees, most of whom were among the more productive, able elements of the population, and who now found themselves herded into the already crowded kingdom of Granada.

Economic hardship, together with population displacement from the urban centres, soon caused revolt in the countryside as well. During the 1260s it was necessary both for Alfonso X of Castile (1252–84) and James I of Aragon to expel the majority of the Muslim farm-workers from their Andalusian and Murcian lands, obliging them either to emigrate to North

56   James I of Aragon and his nobles attend a feast given in their honour by Pedro Martel, captain of the Barcelona galleys. The king sits apart from the nobles and their host. From a mid-fourteenth-century manuscript.

Africa or to Granada. The loss of skilled agricultural workers meant in turn the conversion of rich grain and fruit lands to cattle-grazing. At the same time many of the Christian soldiers who had received farms during the previous two decades re-emigrated to northern Spain, selling their holdings cheaply to the military orders and the war captains, who were already the great landlords of Christian Andalusia. From this period date the great *latifundia* which have been characteristic of southern Spain ever since the middle of the thirteenth century.

Inevitably, one is inclined to compare the great thirteenth-century reconquest of Andalusia with the sixteenth-century conquest of America. In both instances the Christian forces, led by Castile, exhibit the same incredible energy, military prowess and combination of crusading fervour with sheer economic plunder. The gold collected at Las Navas became the basis of the banking ventures of king Sancho the Strong of Navarre, just as the gold of the Incas later enhanced the fortunes of the German bankers of Charles V. What was left of urban real estate in Mexico and Cuzco in the sixteenth century was distributed among the conquerors, as were the houses of Baeza, Ubeda, Jaen and Seville in the thirteenth century. Landed estates, and the labourers to work them, were likewise distributed among the conquerors in both cases. But the nature of the subject population and economy were very different. In both agriculture and urban arts the Muslims of Andalusia were far more advanced than the Christians who conquered them, and the population density of Andalusia was much greater than that of Castile and Leon, whereas in sixteenth-century America the Spaniards conquered lands with a considerably lower population density than that of Andalusia, and with a somewhat less developed economy and technology than that of the conquerors.

In Valencia and Alicante, under the crown of Aragon-Catalonia, the Muslims were exploited economically, although there was not nearly so much population displacement. The chronicle of James I tells us that the king's army was by no means unanimously anxious to occupy the city of Valencia.

57 Country scene, with spoon-making: illustration from Albertus Magnus's *Natural History*.

Priests and crusaders wanted to capture the city, but many of the knights would have preferred to leave it in Muslim hands, to be exploited in time-honoured tributary fashion rather than directly ruled. In any event there was no large-scale population expulsion and no creation of immense estates in Valencia. Rather, the crown distributed individual houses, along with an orchard, a vineyard and anything from three to twelve acres of land. Here, as in the Ebro valley, the Muslim inhabitants continued both as urban craftsmen and as farmers, under Christian overlords. Land units were considerably smaller than in Andalusia, and the technical level, and consequently the traditional prosperity, were much more nearly maintained than in the provinces conquered by Castile. But regardless of the general contrast between Castilian and Aragonese methods, what is

89

most significant is that Christian Spain was unable really to assimilate its rapid military conquests of the years from 1212 to 1248. Not until 1609, with the expulsion of the Moriscos under Philip III, was Christian sovereignty effectively established throughout the rural and mountainous areas of the south, and not even today has the economy of Andalusia recovered from the damage done to it in the thirteenth century.

From the thirteenth century onwards, however, Christian forms of politics, social organization and culture have been dominant in Spain, and Christian ability to exploit, adopt, assimilate or reject various aspects of Islamic and Jewish culture has determined the nature of Spanish civilization down to at least the mid-eighteenth century. Nor has this rich medieval heritage of Christian, Hebrew and Islamic elements ceased by any means to influence the present civilization of Spain. It is, therefore, worth examining in some detail both the separate constituents, and the interactions, of this medieval heritage.

The Christian states, on the eve of the *Reconquista*, were composed overwhelmingly of those who fought, those who prayed and those who tilled the soil. Despite their fluid frontiers, their internal dynastic quarrels and their relative lack of urban life, they were gradually developing political institutions of a constitutional and power-sharing nature. They were all secular monarchies in which the kings not only accepted but extolled the religious authority of the Roman Catholic priesthood, and in which the church supported the temporal authority of the kings. Since clerics were the only literate class in society, they wielded great influence as advisers and diplomats, an influence which was increased further by their role as transmitters of French agricultural and building methods.

But there was a clear distinction between supreme religious and supreme secular authority, so that Christian kings were never the objects of anything resembling emperor-worship. Their authority depended upon the degree of legitimacy in their hereditary claims, and upon the ability and energy with which they performed their political and military tasks. They might

58 A king receives the homage of his vassals: from a late fourteenth-century manuscript.

claim to rule by the Grace of God, but they never claimed to partake of divinity, and their subjects did not prostrate themselves at royal audiences. In theory always, and often in practice, the caliph, and the more presumptuous of the *taifa* kings, were the absolute arbiters of all questions religious and political. But the Christian king was always an obedient son of the church, and was always expected to recognize legal limits upon his secular authority. In contrast also with Muslim practice, the Christian monarchies tended increasingly to accept primogeniture as the rule of succession. This did not prevent frequent civil war among the heirs to a Christian throne, but the situation was somewhat less unstable than in the Muslim kingdoms, where any number of sons by several different mothers might be equally legitimate contestants for the throne.

Frontier conditions, and relative underpopulation, favoured the development of legal rights for the less privileged social castes. During the twelfth century conditions of serfdom were steadily lifted in the older kingdoms of Galicia, Leon, Navarre and Aragon, and they hardly existed for the tough, sturdy peasants of Castile. Women retained property rights in their own dowries and frequently managed the landed interests of their absent warrior-husbands. Church emphasis on monogamy, in contrast with the social institutions of Islam, implied legal, and in many ways practical, equality between the sexes. In order to hold and repopulate their expanding territories, the kings granted legal charters, *fueros*, to the founders of new towns. Such charters always included the right to form a city council with jurisdiction over the surrounding rural area, with control of local taxes and militia, with rights of trial, and with liberty of domicile. Sometimes mayors and judges were locally elected, sometimes they were named by the king, and sometimes the city government was divided between royal and locally chosen officials. The charters vary in detail, and there is no sure way of knowing how closely the actual government corresponded with the legal prescriptions, but clearly the tendency was towards the rule of law, with division of power and explicit definitions of rights and jurisdictions.

The beginnings of parliamentary institutions also date from the late twelfth century. The first Cortes of which we have record met in 1188 in Leon, with separate representation for the nobility, the clergy and the municipalities. By the mid-thirteenth century there were Cortes meeting in Leon, Castile, Aragon and Catalonia. They were called at the king's discretion for the purpose of voting taxes, and the kings frequently used both municipal governments and Cortes to court bourgeois opinion and to counterbalance the predominant influence of the nobles in national policy. In the course of the thirteenth century municipalities also developed their own militias (*Hermandades* in

Castile, *Comunidades* in Aragon) to supplement (or rival) the armies belonging to the king, the great nobles, or the military orders. The peaceful elaboration of such institutions pointed towards constitutional government with a wide dispersion of power. The rivalries and jurisdictional conflicts between them gave rise to the constant political tension and frequent civil war which characterized the medieval centuries. The sense of political participation, along with the economic opportunities accompanying expansion, must have contributed substantially to the extraordinary energy of the Christian kingdoms. In the long centuries of combined symbiosis and conflict with al-Andalus, one of the decisive advantages of Christian Spain was its development of a more democratic, constitutionally structured, and less arbitrary form of politics than prevailed in the Muslim states.

But war and economic factors severely limited the constitutional trends. In the twelfth century the frontier lands of Extremadura and New Castile had already been awarded to the military orders, which ruled their immense estates, in effect, as independent principalities. In the Ebro valley, during the same century, the expanding kingdom of Aragon acquired a large subject population, both urban and rural, and there was no question of political representation for Muslims, although from an economic point of view they frequently received favourable treatment from their Christian overlords. The *fuero* tradition remained strongest in the mountainous northern provinces of Asturias, Navarre and Upper Aragon, and on the plateau of Old Castile, areas in which geographical isolation and the almost 100 per cent Christian population favoured local autonomy and social equality. On the east coast of Spain, the city of Barcelona became one of the great commercial and naval powers in the Mediterranean. It developed virtually as a city-state, governed by an oligarchy of wealthy bourgeois who denied effective representation to both the lower classes and the surrounding peasantry, until social revolution in the fifteenth century forced them to make concessions.

In the early thirteenth century, just before the swift conquest of Andalusia and the Levant coast, the crown of Castile ruled over perhaps three million souls, and that of Aragon over some half million. The conquest of Andalusia added some 300,000 (10 per cent) to the population of Castile. By occupying Valencia, Aragon suddenly increased its population by some 150,000 (30 per cent), of whom the vast majority were Muslims. In 1270, that is to say, after the peasant revolts which had led to the deportation of thousands of Muslims to either Africa or Granada, the Christian population of Valencia and Murcia still amounted to only about 20 per cent of the total. Under such circumstances there was no question of introducing the northern-type municipal *fueros* or Cortes representation. The best land in Andalusia was granted to war captains, and these grants became the basis of the cattle and grain *latifundia* which have dominated that part of Spain ever since. In Murcia and Valencia the estates were smaller, but the continuing presence

RURAL LIFE

59 Peasant ploughing.   60 Ploughing, dairy-far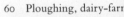

of a large Muslim majority posed a constant threat to Christian rule. Generally speaking, in the lands acquired during the twelfth and thirteenth centuries, military organization, crusading fervour, a ranching economy (in Extremadura, New Castile and parts of Andalusia), or an agricultural economy based upon the labour of a subject caste (the Ebro valley, Valencia and Murcia), all combined with a sense of Christian superiority to hamper the development of the rudimentary constitutionalism of northern Spain.

Social structure and class lines now varied greatly within different portions of the crown lands of the two great kingdoms of Castile and Aragon. Let us first take the crown of Castile. In the north lay the well-watered, forested provinces of Galicia and the Cantabrican mountains. Here a society of small farmers, woodmen and fishermen lived in relatively isolated small communities. The Santiago pilgrimage and the development of the wool export trade to England and Flanders provided

pruning and bee-keeping.   61   Sheep-grazing, as depicted on an altarpiece.

95

some traffic with the outside world. Monasteries, mostly Cistercian, spread French and Roman cultural influences among their immediate neighbours. But for the most part people here experienced a very traditional, settled, locally autonomous life. The population was quite homogeneous, with very few Mozarabs, Jews or Muslims. There were some French immigrants, especially in the twelfth century, but these were generally assimilated very rapidly, having arrived with the same religion, and a language and style of life very similar, to those of their new environment.

On the southern slopes of the Cantabrican chain, and across the *meseta* of Leon and Old Castile, existed a society dominated by herdsmen and farmers. The towns were small, but functionally important in the process of extending and repopulating the frontier. They were largely self-governing, under *fueros* granted by kings who valued them as political counterweights to the nobility. What little artisan work and commerce they engaged in tended to be handled by Mozarabs or Jews. In the introduction of 'consumer goods' to the area, the annual trade fairs in the main towns were more significant than any manufacture carried out in Leon and Castile.

Further south, in the provinces of Toledo, Badajoz and La Mancha, the military orders dominated, with their immense frontier estates devoted to the raising of cattle as well as sheep. The ancient city of Toledo, now the home of an important school of translators, and with its traditionally sizable Mozarab, Jewish and Muslim quarters, lived a far more cosmopolitan, artistic and intellectual life than did the other towns of the *meseta*. With the exception of Toledo, cultural horizons were as narrow as in the north, the social and economic gap between large and small landholders greater, and the spread of rudimentary democracy checked by the power of the orders. Finally, in Andalusia, land, by the late thirteenth century, was very heavily concentrated in the hands of the new nobility created by the period of rapid conquest. Both city life and the agricultural economy had decayed with the large-scale expulsions of Muslim inhabitants, but there were still significant Muslim, and also Jewish, communities, making the social complexion of Andalusia markedly different from that of both Old and New Castile.

Wide contrasts prevailed in the territories of the crown of Aragon also. The Pyrenean valleys of Upper Aragon and the mountainous interior of Catalonia were inhabited by a traditionalist, isolated, relatively homogeneous society of small farmers. They had had more contact with France than had the communities of Galicia and Leon, but otherwise were similar in composition and way of life. As they expanded south and east along the Ebro they became the masters of a technically skilled Muslim population which had irrigated and cultivated that valley for four centuries. Perhaps because the Christians were few in number, perhaps because their political and military resources were heavily engaged in southern France, perhaps because they had been accustomed to the physical proximity of the Muslim community (there being no wide, almost empty plateau between the mountain towns and the valley), the Aragonese did not expel the Muslims, but simply governed and exploited them. They followed a similar policy when expanding into Valencia and along the Mediterranean coast, so that the kingdom of Aragon, throughout the later Middle Ages, contained a much higher proportion of Muslims, both farmers and city-dwellers, than did Castile.

Meanwhile, Barcelona, and to a lesser degree, Tortosa, developed steadily as commercial centres. Coastal Catalonia was from the beginning of the Muslim era the natural corridor for both commercial and cultural contact between al-Andalus and western Europe. Catalan churches had been governed by the archbishop of Narbonne. Neither the Mozarabic rite, nor frontier-type *fueros*, nor military orders had ever exercised any influence here. The language was closer to Provençal than to Castilian, and French forms of landholding, family and business organization spread naturally to Catalonia. By the twelfth century a strong native bourgeoisie had developed. Catalan shipping rivalled that of the Italian cities, and was increasingly important in the trade with North African ports. When the Catalans reconquered Majorca in 1229 they expelled the Muslim farmers and settled veterans of the campaign on the expropriated lands. As in the case of Andalusia, the combination of the military dangers of the frontier with the need to reward soldiers and sailors probably determined the expulsion policy.

The social result of these several developments was that the crown of Aragon governed at least three very different societies: a traditional, Christian rural society in the north; a prosperous, considerably urbanized society of Christians ruling over a Muslim majority in the lower Ebro and on the Levant coast; and in coastal Catalonia an aggressive, commercial and naval society containing very few Muslims, and possessing the only sizable Christian bourgeoisie anywhere in Spain. Even though the population and territory of Aragon-Catalonia were much smaller than those of Castile, there were separate Cortes for Aragon, Catalonia and Valencia. This development reflected both the extremely heterogeneous character of the dynastic holdings, and the lesser military energy of a crown which was deeply involved in French politics, and which had to grant virtually independent, city-state, status to Barcelona and its hinterland.

The governments of both kingdoms lacked the information and the skilled personnel to rule their heterogeneous dominions. They each suffered from repeated internal dynastic struggles. Aragon was deeply involved in French and Mediterranean affairs. Castile dreamt of conquering North Africa and of absorbing Portugal. Once the military reconquest of the peninsula had been completed, with the deliberate exception of Granada, the wealthy families and the military orders turned their bellicose energies on one another. The nobility, on grounds of their military functions, claimed exemption from taxation, and demanded that the responsible government jobs be given to them, rather than to the small and despised bourgeoisie. Someone had to manage the sale of wool, the upkeep of forests and dry farmed estates, the care of large flocks, the supply of arms, the organization of trade fairs, the import and payment for luxuries. Someone had to have an approximate idea of the forms and extent of wealth available in different parts of the country, someone had to collect taxes, someone had to negotiate with nations which did not speak Castilian.

For the performance of these functions, exception made for the city-state of Barcelona, both kingdoms depended heavily upon the Jews. It is by no means easy to estimate the size of the medieval Jewish community. Professors Jaime Vicens Vives and Jorge Nadal, the most careful demographic historians of Spain up to the present, use a figure of 200,000 for the year 1391 (at which time the great persecutions and forced conversions began), and they speak of the reconquest of Andalusia as possibly adding 100,000 Jews to the crown of Castile. But the great Jewish historian Yitzhak Baer tells us that the tax rolls of Castile in 1290 show only 3,600 tax-paying Jewish families in the whole kingdom, which would suggest an upper limit of perhaps 20,000 Jews for Castile; since Castile was about six times as populous as Aragon-Catalonia, the total for all of Spain could hardly, extrapolating from this information, have reached 22,000. Besides which, according to Baer, there were practically no Jews in the cities of Andalusia at the time of their occupation in the 1240s. Vicens and Nadal also believe that, from the late twelfth to the early fifteenth century, the population of Spain approximately doubled, from three to six millions in the case of Castile, from 500,000 to 1,000,000 in the case of Aragon. If we make the reasonable assumption that the Jewish population also doubled in this period, such an assumption could in no way account for a jump from 20,000 to 200,000. In addition, it is as well to remember that both the Vicens-Nadal and the Baer estimates are open to challenge. Thus it would be more misleading than helpful to offer any numerical estimate. The significant point is that the Jews played a role in medieval Spain far out of proportion to their numbers, a role which can be described, and partially explained.

Jewish communities had existed in the Levant and Andalusia at least from early Roman times. They had been persecuted by the Visigoths, and on the whole had preferred to live under Muslim rule from 711 to about 1100. The emirs and caliphs of Cordoba, and the *taifa* kings, had almost all followed the enlightened Muslim policy of toleration for the 'Peoples of the Book', i.e. the Jews and the Christians, whose religions were thought of as stages on the road to the final revelation which had been given to Muhammad. Muslim law treated the Jews and Christians as separate communities with considerable internal autonomy in the administration of taxes, justice, sanitation, commercial regulations, etc. The sovereigns of the small Christian states in the early Middle Ages imitated this Islamic practice, and so, from the beginning, the *aljamas* of Leon, Castile, Navarre, Aragon and Catalonia controlled the internal administration of their villages and were collectively responsible for taxes levied by the crown.

As long as Muslim rule remained tolerant, the great majority of Spanish Jews lived in al-Andalus. But after about 1100 Almoravid and Almohad intolerance, together with the significant economic growth of the Christian kingdoms, had made northern Spain more attractive than al-Andalus. In the occupation of Toledo (1085) Alfonso VI had confirmed the existing rights of self-government enjoyed by the Muslim, Mozarabic and Jewish communities of that city. In the Ebro valley and the Levant, the new Christian rulers during the twelfth century valued and protected the middle-class functions performed by both Jews and Muslims. In Old Castile and the north the Jews faced a degree of prejudice as 'outsiders' and 'city slickers' among a sober farming population, but there were no restrictions on their right to hold land or to engage in any occupations they chose.

In relation to the Christian community the Jews were proportionately more urban in their occupations; but in view of widespread prejudice even today, the emphasis belongs on the word proportionately. They appear typically in the *aljama* records as weavers, tanners, shoemakers, dyers, carpenters, blacksmiths, saddlers, furriers, potters. Local *fueros* also specified lands which were either owned or farmed on a rental basis by Jews. Relatively few Jews were full-time soldiers, but Jewish communities living on monastic lands or those of the military orders often held frontier fortresses and had their taxes reduced for military service, just as did Christians performing similar services. Class gradations within the Jewish community were less marked than among the Christians, however, since they had no hereditary nobility and no military caste.

Jewish community life, like that of its Castilian neighbours, was marked by sober, austere standards. Marriages were usually arranged early, and without romantic courtship. Divorce policies were less liberal than those of Talmudic Palestine. There were severe penalties for adultery, and bastardy was rare. Masters were made to marry their concubines, and polygamy was tolerated, but rare. As in Christian Spain generally, there was plenty of private violence despite severe laws and punishments. In distinction from Christian Spain there was strong community support for education, and the literacy rate was much higher among Jews than among Christians. In the twelfth and early thirteenth century severe social tensions accompanied the northward migration of the Andalusian Jews, whose sophisticated urban culture made them look upon their northern coreligionists as yokels. Wealthy Andalusian Jews, whose services were doubly valuable to the kings because of their knowledge of Arabic and of Islamic politics, were frequently exempted from the legal jurisdiction and the collective tax responsibilities of the local *aljamas*. Needless to say, such privileges caused bitter jealousy. The rabbis of northern Spain also objected vehemently to the intellectual influence of Maimonides, claiming that the rationalism of his *Guide to the Perplexed* was undermining the faith of the orthodox.

Alfonso X, who was the first sovereign to rule a Castile which stretched from the Cantabrican ports to the tip of Andalusia, liked to style himself the 'King of the Three Religions'.

His father-in-law, James I of Aragon, was also equally solicitous for the welfare of his subjects of all three religions, and
their successors in the fourteenth century generally affirmed
similar intentions. This was a matter of both personal enlightenment and political necessity. European as well as Muslim legal
conceptions treated the religious communities as separate bodies
owing allegiance to a common king, but not held together by
any 'national' bond. The Jews, a very small minority never
amounting, by the highest estimates, to more than 4 per cent of
the population, were literally the property of the crown. It was
in the interest of the king to protect that property as he would
any other valuables; conversely, at times of revolt against the
king, armed rebels would attack the Jews as a way of attacking
the king.

Quite aside from their availability as crown property, the
Jews were the natural intermediaries between Muslim and
Christian Spain. The educated among them often spoke both
Arabic and Castilian, and many Jews had family connections
in both parts of Spain. Perhaps more important: at the intuitive,

102

64 A domestic Passover service.

62 Far left, a fortified
Jewish house in Toledo
reflects the insecurity
almost always felt by Jews.

63 Left, a fourteenth-century
Jew wears the distinctive
sign of his religion
on his chest.

non-verbal, level Jewish culture occupied an intermediate position between that of the Muslim south and the Christian north. The Jews resembled the Christians in their emphasis on monogamy, their communal anxiety about intermarriage, their stress on the virtues of work and sobriety and the greater dignity they accorded women in their laws and social customs. They resembled the Muslims in their urban culture, their artisan skills, their philosophical speculations, their scientific and scholarly pursuits. Certain elements in the church, and the fervour generated by the crusades, always constituted a latent threat of persecution. But in the eleventh and twelfth century the Jews were not subjected to legal disabilities in Christian Spain.

During the thirteenth century contradictory currents prevailed. On the one hand the majority of ordinary Jews continued the artisan and agricultural functions which had long been characteristic of them. They also participated in the reconquest of Andalusia, and were rewarded with land and houses, just as were the Christian participants. But the Albigensian crusade in France, and the rise of the mendicant orders, produced a new wave of intolerance within the church itself. Pope Innocent III and his successors multiplied their warnings to the kings of Aragon and Castile not to trust the Jews, and the Dominican friars called insistently for mass conversions. But toleration was both traditional and necessary for the Spanish sovereigns, and so, while they made verbal, and even legal, concessions to the pressure of the church militant, they continued on the whole to employ Jewish officials and to protect the established Jewish communities.

Perhaps the most valued field of Jewish service to Christian sovereigns and lords was finance. Here too, because of deeply rooted anti-Semitic traditions based upon ignorance and false emphasis, it is essential to understand the entire context. The church forbade Christians to lend money to one another for interest. The Talmud laid a similar prohibition upon Jews with regard to their co-religionists. But Jews and Christians were free to lend money to each other. It was customary for Jews,

Christians and Muslims as well to form partnerships in order to be able to invest in, and share the profits of, each other's business ventures without engaging in 'usury'. It was equally customary, in cases where businessmen found it absolutely necessary to lend money to their co-religionists, for a Christian to act as broker for a loan between Jews and for a Jew to act as broker for a loan between Christians.

The need for loans at interest was well recognized. The rates were indeed usurious by modern standards. The Cortes of Barcelona in the thirteenth century fixed the maximum at 20 per cent, and under Alfonso X the Castilian rate stood at 33 per cent. The relatively lower Catalan rate reflects the greater commercial development of Catalonia in comparison with Castile, but the lack of stable currency, of safe roads or shipping lanes and of sure legal recourse in case of theft, accounts for the steep percentages in comparison with modern bank rates. Christians, including clerics, lent money at interest. There was nothing about either the practice or the rates which was distinctively Jewish.

The military orders and the great landed magnates frequently employed Jews to supervise both the general economy and the financial needs of their estates. The kings, having nothing resembling a bureau of internal revenue, depended upon tax-farming – the practice of contracting with an individual who would collect taxes on behalf of the king, and receive an agreed commission payment for such service. A high proportion of the tax-farmers was Jewish, not because the kings so desired, but because, as they frequently complained, Christians did not offer themselves as candidates for this dangerous and unpopular occupation. It seems also to be true, on the basis of scattered records (which are nevertheless consistent with each other), that the Jewish communities paid a very high proportion of the total taxes collected by the kings of Castile and Aragon. Thus the tax registers of the crown of Aragon for the year 1294 indicate that the Jews paid 22 per cent of all the taxes collected. The Jews could not have constituted more than 3 to 4 per cent of the population, nor does the register include special levies such as those for diplomatic missions, royal journeys and marriages, etc.

Financial transactions led naturally to other forms of social contact between Christians and Jews. Jews were often godfathers and baptismal witnesses for Christian associates, and Christians frequently witnessed circumcisions and marriages. In small towns as well as among wealthy families, business contracts and wills were often notarized by both a Jewish and a Christian official. Among the wealthiest families of both communities intermarriage became increasingly frequent from the thirteenth century onwards, a practice frowned on by the religious authorities and by the common man in both communities.

The Jews in Spain might prosper, and might enjoy close business and personal relations with Christians, but they could never feel truly secure. In the late twelfth century Almohad raids along the frontier were often attributed to Jewish intrigues, and resulted in violence against the *aljamas*. When Alfonso IX of Leon died in 1230, resistance to the reunification of Leon and Castile included attacks on the Jews, in this case accused of supporting Castilian centralism. The thirteenth-century kings vacillated in their policies. James I of Aragon considered himself a friend of the Jews, a tolerant and enlightened sovereign. When he occupied the kingdom of Valencia he granted important trading concessions in grain, oil and cattle to the Jews, and allowed them to retain their own quarter in the capital city. Jewish farmers in the Levant, like their Christian counterparts, depended on the labour of Muslim serfs. One of the ways that such serfs could become free men was to become Christians. The king heeded the request of the Jewish landlords to curb the proselytizing efforts of the church and to make manumission more difficult. But in 1254 (the same year in which Louis IX of France, newly returned from the crusade, expelled the Jews and cancelled all debts to them) James confiscated for the crown all debts owed to the Jews of Aragon, 'for the salvation of our soul', and to punish alleged violations of royal edicts.

Alfonso X of Castile also considered himself a friend of the Jews, awarding land, houses and mills to Toledo Jews in the resettlement of Seville, and treating the local Andalusian Jews as if they were Christians. But his policies were inconsistent, to say the least. In Murcia, where the Muslim population was large and restive, and where he could surely have used the co-operation of a satisfied Jewish community, he did not permit Jews to reside in the Christian quarter of the city. Legislation written under his direction included restrictions on business dealings between Jews and Christians, though no serious attempt was made to enforce such restrictions. One of the great Jewish civil servants of the time, Solomon Ibn Zadok of Toledo, had collected the tribute of Granada for Ferdinand III and been the chief tax-collector for Alfonso X. When he died in 1273 all his real estate and accumulated goods in Seville warehouses were confiscated for the benefit of the cathedral of Seville.

No permanent dishonour may have been intended. Solomon's son Isaac, known in Castilian as D. Zag de la Maleha, also served as chief tax-farmer. But when royal funds were lost during the civil war between Alfonso X and his son, the future Sancho IV, the king was quick to see Jewish treason. Thus, in 1278, he ordered D. Zag to deliver a large sum of money to the Alfonsine forces besieged in Algeciras. When the partisans of prince Sancho got hold of the money, Alfonso imprisoned all the Jewish tax-farmers of Castile. D. Zag himself was hanged, and a group of wealthy Sevillian Jews were held hostage in their synagogue until they could raise a ransom of some 4,380,000 *maravedis* (twice the total annual contributions normally collected from the *aljamas* of Castile). Doubtless both James I and Alfonso X saw no inconsistency in their behaviour. They felt nothing but admiration and friendship for Jews who were their faithful servants, and who contributed signally to the prosperity of their domains. But as the church ceaselessly emphasized, Jews could never be completely trusted, and their transgressions must be sternly punished by a king responsible for the material and spiritual welfare of three religious communities.

107

65 A page from the Astronomical Tables of king Peter IV, showing tables and figures of the constellation of the Bear.

Besides their important economic functions the Jews at the court of Alfonso X played an essential role in the development of Spanish literary and intellectual life. The Jews of Christian Spain did not produce great creative figures of their own in the thirteenth century. Rather, they offered to Castile and Aragon the entire heritage of Islamic and Hebrew culture, as it had flourished steadily in al-Andalus from the ninth to the twelfth century. King Alfonso was much interested in astronomy and applied science, and in history, in so far as it might contribute to the glory of Castile and to his hopes of becoming Holy Roman Emperor. He was interested also in Roman law, especially since it might be used in the codification of the disparate *fueros*, and might enhance the prestige and authority of the monarchy rather than the local nobility. The Jews had already translated the Old Testament into Castilian, making it in some ways the language of their spiritual life, whereas the Christians were still using only Latin for such purposes.

66　The *Tablas Alfonsinas:* gold reliquary, in the form of a triptych, given to Seville Cathedral by Alfonso X in 1284.

The Jewish development of Castilian as an intellectual vehicle, together with their knowledge of Arabic and Hebrew, made them eager collaborators of a sovereign enthusiastic to make learned works available to his people in their own language. Jewish scholars, compilers and editors played a role comparable with that of the *philosophes* of eighteenth-century France. They translated into Castilian the major astronomical, mathematical, botanical, medical and philosophical works of the Arab world. The famous *Alphonsine Tables* were the work of two Jewish astronomers, who dedicated their book to the king, and who told him that his reign should be considered the start of a new era, just as the Greeks had based their chronology on the reign of Alexander, and the Romans theirs on the rule of Caesar. French and Italian scholars were imported to translate major Latin works, and to collaborate on the *Grande e General Estoria* which was the first national history published in a European vernacular language. As the great twentieth-century

67 The Corinthian column:
a marble capital from
Medinat al-Zahira.

Spanish scholar Americo Castro has pointed out, Castilian became, through the collaboration of Alfonso X and the Jews of his court, the natural vehicle for a high intellectual culture combining the heritages of Islam, Judaism and Romano-Germanic Europe.

The most striking example of the Spanish medieval genius for fruitful synthesis of the three cultures occurs in the fields of architecture, sculpture and the decorative arts. The emirs of Cordoba early set an example of eclecticism and of complete freedom from ethnic or religious limitations in their notions of art. In their palaces they used the Corinthian columns, the geometric decorations and the stone mosaics which the first Islamic conquerors had seen in occupying much of the Hellenistic world. They adopted the keyhole arch from the Visigoths, and Abd-al-Rahman II, in the portion of the Great Mosque of Cordoba which he built in about 850, used two rows of Roman arches superimposed on one another in precisely the style of the Roman aqueduct at Merida. The only limitation on these borrowings from Roman, Byzantine and Visigothic traditions was the avoidance of human representation in accordance with the Islamic and Jewish prohibitions on images.

Between the eighth and the tenth century al-Andalus developed a syncretic artistic style with clear traits of its own. Islamic artists were more concerned with decoration than with architecture, with abstract design than with colour. They could disguise the most beautiful stone by covering it with a maze of intricate sculpture, a coat of plaster, or both. Their abstract and floral designs were purposely unrealistic. Their sense of beauty depended more upon elegant lines and proportions, careful relationships between figures and their background spacing, than upon originality of design. In the tenth century they added the lobed arch to their repertoire, again for decorative rather than architectural purposes. In the ninth and tenth century they also developed in their Andalusian workshops the same type of beautiful textiles and the same high quality of ivory, pottery and metallic artisanware that was characteristic of the Abbasid empire in the East.

During these same centuries a pre-Romanesque, or Asturian, style of church architecture evolved, characterized by rectangular stone construction, Roman arches and sculptured columns. But there was no exchange of influences between this style and the Islamic. Only the tenth-century Mozarabic churches of Leon and Castile show a consciousness of Islamic trends. They have

68   The Mozarabic style: view of the interior of San Miguel de Escalada, notable for its Visigothic arches.

the same thin double columns which give a wonderful sense of interior space to the Great Mosque of Cordoba, and like many Arab villas they were placed so as to gain maximum aesthetic advantage of the landscape. But in general the Mozarabic style avoided Oriental elements in favour of strict Roman-Visigothic tradition.

The great symbiosis and synthesis of art styles began in the late eleventh century and lasted well into the sixteenth. The first of its constituent elements was the Romanesque, imported from Languedoc (because of its immediate contiguity) and from Burgundy (as a result of the immigration of the architects and artisans who arrived with the Cluniac monks). French Romanesque churches were built usually of stone, though sometimes of brick. They were characterized by thick, heavy walls, a low nave and square bell-towers. The interior stone columns were decorated with painted sculpture illustrating scenes from the Bible, and from the lives of Christ and the saints. Romanesque churches appeared first in Catalonia and Navarre, and then during the twelfth century spread rapidly across northern Spain along the route to Santiago.

The second major element, dating from the later twelfth century, was represented by the distinctive Cistercian architecture, which combined the pointed arch and the high nave of contemporary French Gothic with the familiar Romanesque.

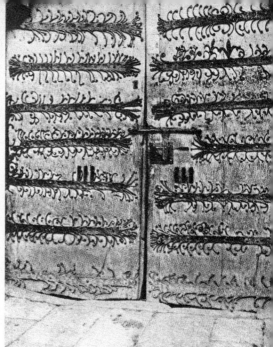

69 Cloisters at the monastery of Santa Maria de Ripoll, completed in 1032 (opposite).

70, 71 Nave (above left) and Romanesque doors (above right) of the abbey church, Meira.

72 Portico of San Lorenzo de Carboeiro, enlivened by monks playing musical instruments (below left).

73 Sculptured west façade of the main portal of Santa Maria de Ripoll (below right).

Cistercian communities were larger than the earlier Cluniac ones. They had thick outer walls, apses of the Romanesque type and a high nave, whose supporting columns were usually not sculpted, possibly from motives of economy and speed of construction, or perhaps simply because of the absence of the imaginative stone-cutters who had worked for Cluny. It is sometimes said that the Cistercians avoided Biblical sculpture from motives of spiritual austerity, but there is no lack of decoration and aesthetic sensitivity in their buildings. Many of them had magnificently sculptured wooden doors and roofs, and their cloisters frequently had beautifully decorated rows of thin double columns. This carpentry and column decoration was the work of Mudejar rather than French craftsmen, and testifies to the growing self-confidence of Christian Spain and its readiness to employ the services, and adopt the artistic styles, of its Muslim subjects.

The third key element in the synthesis was the Mudejar style itself. The Mudejars were those Muslims who lived under Christian rule. They were numerous from the twelfth century in the Ebro valley, and they constituted a large proportion of the population in all the territories acquired by Castile and Aragon in the thirteenth century. After the fall of the caliphate there was a great flowering of Islamic architecture in the *taifa* kingdoms. Few of its monuments survived the reconquest, but a building such as the Alfajeria of Saragossa indicates clearly that techniques of geometric and floral design, and craftsmanship in wood, metal and ceramics, achieved an even higher level of virtuosity in the eleventh century than had been witnessed at Cordoba in the tenth. Local Muslim rulers had competed with one another in architecture, just as they had rivalled each other as patrons of poetry.

The artistic skills of these Muslim workers were suddenly and cheaply available to the new Christian rulers. Mudejar art, sumptuous when used to build royal residences such as the palace of Maria de Padilla in Tordesillas or the Alcazar of Seville, could be simple, and regionally inspired, when used to build small churches and modest residences. Brick construction was combined with Romanesque architecture in many a small church in Aragon. Mudejar brickwork, like the earlier Islamic sculpture, was notable for beauty of line and proportion, and for the development of the blind arches, which decorated and broke up the rectangular surfaces of Romanesque walls and towers. Mudejar craftsmen also supplied sculpted doors and roofs, colourfully tiled walls and floors, sculpted furniture, rich textile hangings and quality ceramics in accordance with the taste and the wealth of the builder. Inexpensiveness of building materials and labour, and the adaptability of brick to practically all the architectural needs of the time, made for the rapid diffusion, the variety and the longevity of the Mudejar style. The beauty and the variety produced by this synthesis of Romanesque, Cistercian and Mudejar styles can be seen all over Castile and Aragon to this day, and constitutes a happy synthesis not lastingly achieved in other aspects of Spanish cultural life.

74, 75 Left, the thirteenth-century church of San Lorenzo, Sahagun. Right, the Alcazar of Seville, commissioned by Christians, but constructed by Muslims.

IV VITALITY AND CHAOS IN THE
LATER MIDDLE AGES

The last two centuries of the Middle Ages in Spain, from the late thirteenth to the late fifteenth, were marked by economic and cultural vitality, and by political instability which frequently eventuated in civil war. In its economic vitality Spain was sharing in the general recovery of the Mediterranean and west European world. From the eighth to the eleventh century the Mediterranean had been dominated by Islam. With the exception of trade and cultural relations with al-Andalus, Europe had been largely isolated from Africa and the Orient. The crusades were, among other things, a sign of the re-awakened vitality, of the demographic, and later economic, expansiveness of Europe from the beginning of the eleventh century. The crusades to the Holy Land, and to a lesser but still considerable degree, the reconquest in the Iberian peninsula, required the transport and supply of large numbers of men. Such transport, to Anatolia and Palestine, was made possible by the commercial revolution in Italy, and the traffic to the Near East encouraged the further development of that commercial revolution not only in Italy, but along the shores of southern France and Catalonia, and in the Rhineland and Flanders.

The commercial revolution of the twelfth century involved the growth, in both numbers and wealth, of a self-governing urban bourgeoisie. In Italy, where central power was weak and where pope could be played off against emperor, great cities such as Venice, Florence and Genoa became independent, sovereign, oligarchic republics. In Burgundy, France and Aragon-Catalonia the cities obtained a substantial degree of independence in the form of concessions and privileges from the kings, but remained under royal sovereignty. In the development of cities and the revival of Mediterranean trade the crown

76 The Consulado del Mar (Consulate of the Sea) in session: from an early fifteenth-century manuscript.

of Aragon played a much larger role than did that of Castile. It therefore makes sense, in describing the economic history of later medieval Spain, to begin with Aragon.

The kingdom of Aragon-Catalonia was a purely dynastic union dating from the marriage, in 1137, of count Ramon Berenguer IV of Barcelona to Petronilla, the infant daughter of king Ramiro of Aragon. The two peoples spoke different languages, had different laws and maintained separate Cortes. They were united by common political interests in southern France and in the reconquest of the Ebro valley and of Valencia. Barcelona had a long tradition of handling trade between Cordoba and southern France. The church of Catalonia had been attached to the archbishopric of Narbonne. French traders and farmers had settled in large numbers in Catalonia during the eleventh and twelfth centuries, and Barcelona supplied arms and money to support the campaigns of the king of Aragon in Languedoc. In the thirteenth century, however, the crown of Aragon turned its main attention from southern France to the Mediterranean. King Peter II was killed in 1213 at the battle of Muret, near Toulouse. His successors, James I and Peter III

77 The marriage of Ramon Berenguer IV to Petronilla, as illustrated in the genealogical tree of the monastery of Poblet.

118

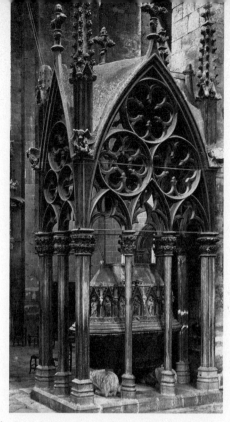

78 The tomb of Peter III in the monastery of Santa Cruz.

(1276–85), both devoted their reigns to Mediterranean expansion, as can be seen from the following key dates: 1230, conquest of Majorca; 1238, occupation of Valencia; 1258, treaty of Corbeil, renouncing territorial ambitions in France; the 1260s, co-operation with Castile in subduing Murcia; 1282, conquest of Sicily; 1286, conquest of Minorca; 1297, first foothold in Sardinia.

From the late twelfth to the mid-fifteenth century Barcelona became incontestably the greatest city in Spain and one of the leading Mediterranean cities, rivalling Genoa and Florence in the volume of its trade and the power of its combined merchant marine navy. The city was virtually self-governing under a royal charter of the king of Aragon. A 'Council of 100', chosen from among the upper bourgeoisie, and renewing its membership in the manner of a modern corporation, supervised the apportionment and collection of taxes, the prices of essential food supplies, the maintenance of roads, warehouses and ship-yards, and the condition of the landing beach (there being no jetty-protected harbours in those days). The city dominated the neighbouring countryside. Commercial capital came from the profits of farming and land sales, the rising value of urban real estate and the city's far-flung commerce. Barcelona's virtual independence resulted more from its financial power and foreign trade than from the rights and privileges of the royal charter. Through municipal taxation it collected far more revenue than did the crown. The city also borrowed money through bond issues, and its funded debt thus became both a supplementary source of venture capital and a source of profit to the bondholders.

Inevitably, the city engaged in considerable overland trade and in manufacture as well as commerce. It was necessary to bring wheat, olive oil, wine, dairy products and lumber from distances of sixty miles and more, and to transport iron from the Pyrenees. The textile industry developed early. In the fourteenth century Barcelona already produced arms, wrought iron, textiles and leather goods. It manufactured everything necessary to ships: seasoned planks and masts, cordage, sails, anchors, nails and the carts and harnesses needed to transport its manufactures. Its artisans were organized in guilds which protected the professional interests of each group, and which were supervised generally by the municipal government. Entrance standards to such guilds were exacting. Apprentice-ship for silversmiths lasted six years; for tailors and carpenters, four; for cloth manufacturers, three.

Along with Genoa, Barcelona was the largest shipbuilder in the Mediterranean during the thirteenth and fourteenth centuries. The city constructed four-ton, thirty-foot-long ships for the coastal trade; twenty- to fifty-ton ships for the triangular run between Barcelona, Valencia and Majorca; and ships of between 100 and 900 tons (averaging between 250 and 500) for trade with North Africa and the Near East. The ships were

79   In distress at sea, sailors pray to the Madonna and Child.

powered by a combination of sails and oars. They were built of wood, and painted brightly, often in the striped red and gold which were the colours of the old county of Barcelona. They carried their own home-manufactured spare ropes, sails and anchors. They could travel at a maximum rate of twelve to thirteen knots per hour, making a typical voyage from Majorca to Tunis in about twenty days, or from Barcelona to Sardinia in about thirty.

Barcelona also developed major diplomatic and legal institutions. In the Muslim cities of North Africa it obtained extra-territorial concessions, *alfondigos*, with a church, bakery, hostel, baths, storehouses and cemetery. Each *alfondigo* was governed by a consul who could act for all citizens of the crown of Aragon. Originally, the consuls were appointed by the king, but after 1266 they were named by the municipal government of Barcelona. The famous Consulado del Mar, the Consulate of the Sea, also originated in thirteenth-century Barcelona. In 1257, the city fathers created a 'University of the Leading Citizens of the Shore' to supervise and police the landing beaches. It quickly acquired two major functions: first to act as a chamber of commerce; and second, to serve as a tribunal for conflicts involving merchants and shipmasters of all nationalities trading in the city. In the latter capacity it developed a body of maritime 'case-law', which became highly influential throughout the Mediterranean world. Similar consulates were established in Valencia in 1283 and in Majorca in 1343. Majorca was important also for a school of Jewish cartographers who produced the *portulanos*, maps showing with great accuracy the nature of the coastlines and indicating the compass courses connecting the major ports.

The ships of the crown of Aragon engaged in an extraordinary variety of trading ventures. Along the Catalan coast they carried Costa Brava coral; wheat from Tortosa at the mouth of the Ebro; kindling, charcoal and lumber from the beaches closest to the forest sources; and of course fish. Along the coast of Languedoc they carried all these products and, additionally, hides, leather, textiles and spices. Indeed the lucrative spice trade of southern France was dominated by the Catalans until well into the fifteenth century. They were also the carriers of Burgundy wine, whose high qualities were developed during the residence of the popes at Avignon in the fourteenth century, and which tended to drive Aragonese wines out of their home market.

Further afield, they exchanged Catalan textiles and coral for Sicilian wheat and Sardinian silver. Naples, then the largest city in Europe, was a principal market for both textiles and for the Sicilian wheat arriving in Catalan ships. Barcelona competed on more or less equal terms with Genoa in the coastal trade along the western shores of Italy. It competed unsuccessfully for a

80   Map of Hispania made by the Jewish cartographer, Iresques of Majorca, 1375.

share of the Byzantine trade. At the same time, during the fourteenth century it also dominated the seaborne trade of Egypt and of several small Muslim principalities on the north coast of Africa: Tunis, Bougie and Tlemcen. Here it delivered

Catalan textiles, ceramics, arms, hides, leather goods and cordage; and much of this merchandise crossed the Sahara to reach the Sudan. Just as Sudanese gold had been the basis of the gold coinage of the caliphate, so it became the basis of Catalan currency in the fourteenth century.

Theoretically, trade with the Muslims was illicit. After the Muslim conquest of St John of Acre in 1291 the pope had issued a bull forbidding trade in arms, food and ships on pain of excommunication. The king of Aragon had then arranged with Rome to establish a special tribunal to grant dispensations to the deserving merchants of the crown, and the latter thought of the operations of this tribunal as one more form of tax. The king profited as well by treaties of the sort signed by James II with the bey of Tunis in 1301, whereby half the customs charges collected in Tunis on the trade of Aragonese subjects was to be returned to the Aragonese treasury. Late in the Middle Ages, particularly in the years between 1380 and 1440, merchants of the crown of Aragon engaged in the slave trade, obtaining their human cargo from both North Africa and the shores of the Black Sea. There was no clear line between trade and piracy in this era. In the late fourteenth century Catalan, Venetian and Genoese ships would sink one another in the fierce competition for the spice and slave trades of the Near East – a fact which was to aid the revival of Muslim naval power in the fifteenth century. But in the days of their maximum prosperity and diplomatic success, the merchants of the crown of Aragon easily dominated the trade of two main sectors of the western Mediterranean: the narrow sea bounded by Majorca, Ibiza and the Levant coastline on the north, and extending from Algiers to Ceuta on the African coast; and the rough quadrilateral bounded by Sardinia, Sicily, Tunis and Bougie. The conquest of Sicily under Peter the Great and the exploits of the Catalan Company in the Peloponnese in the fourteenth century underpinned Catalan commerce in the latter areas.

Finally, Catalan and Valencian merchants played a prominent role in the Atlantic trade. They carried wool, tin, salt pork and

81 Contemporary seal
bearing portrait of
James II of Aragon.

esparto to England and Flanders. Increasingly during the
fourteenth and fifteenth centuries, Valencian agricultural products were prized in northern Europe: oranges, pomegranates,
raisins, filberts, walnuts, almonds and saffron. In return the
merchants brought English and Flemish cloth, of higher quality
than any manufactured then in Spain, and Baltic herring. Their
merchant colonies were important in Seville, Lisbon and
Bruges. Generally speaking the curve of trade prosperity rose
until the European economic crisis of 1381, remained erratic
between 1381 and 1427, and then declined during the remainder
of the fifteenth century. Increased Italian competition, piracy
and a crisis of the Catalan banking and investment system after
1427 are explanations frequently offered for the economic
decline of the crown of Aragon. Whatever the reasons for that
decline, it was certainly one of the unfortunate factors in the
building of Spain's American empire that the discovery of the

125

New World coincided with the decline of Aragonese naval and commercial prowess, and the triumph of Genoese, Florentine and Flemish economic interests.

During the last two centuries of the Middle Ages the economy of the crown of Castile also underwent important development. The commercial revolution did not occur to such a significant degree as in Italy, Aragon-Catalonia and Flanders. There was very little in the way of a confident, aggressive bourgeoisie, competing on favourable terms with the nobility for political influence, and enjoying trade, investment, profit and economic expansion as a way of life just as honourable and adventurous as the life of a soldier or crusader. But Castile was perhaps six times as populous as Aragon-Catalonia. It had led the reconquest, and it was the centre of the vital religious and intellectual life of Spain. After the occupation of Andalusia it consisted of four quite different geographical and social provinces: the Cantabrican mountains and the north coast, thinly populated and engaged in forestry, fishing and shipping; Galicia, Leon and Old Castile, varied in climate and agriculture, but similar in the possession of a conservative society based on the old triumvirate of soldier, priest and farmer, and prizing the local autonomy of its municipal *fueros*; New Castile, La Mancha and Extremadura, the wide, windswept *meseta* dominated by sheep ranching interests and by the military orders, and including a significant Mudejar component in both the urban and rural working class; and Andalusia, semi-tropical in climate, with a large subject Muslim population, dominated by the newly created landed aristocracy.

Throughout this immense and varied territory agriculture remained primitive, producing only for subsistence except in the immediate neighbourhood of the main cities: Burgos, Toledo, Seville. Small-scale artisan industry developed in particular areas during the fourteenth century: shipbuilding in Santander and Seville; mercury-mining near Almaden; arms and ceramics in Toledo, and soap in Andalusia. Low-grade cloth was also produced in Salamanca and Zamora for both local and Portuguese markets.

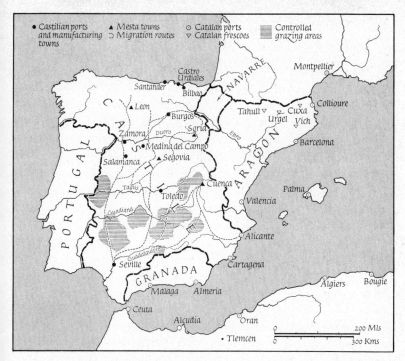

Key:
- ● Castilian ports and manufacturing towns
- ▲ Mesta towns
- ⊃ Migration routes
- ○ Catalan ports
- ▽ Catalan frescoes
- ▨ Controlled grazing areas

82   The economic and artistic life of Spain.

But, overwhelmingly, the economy of late medieval Castile depended upon the production and export of raw wool. While the commercial revolution was occurring in northern Italy and Catalonia, a veritable wool revolution was taking place in Castile. Territorial expansion had greatly increased the grazing area available by the end of the thirteenth century. Demographic increases in Spain and western Europe meant that there were more people to be clothed, and rising prosperity meant that more of those people could afford more and better clothes. England had been the great wool-supplier of the previous century, but her wool trade had suffered from her continual wars on the Continent. Meanwhile, shortly before 1300, the particularly sturdy North African merino sheep was introduced into Andalusia and successfully crossbred with native strains.

127

As a result of the coincidence of these several factors Castile suddenly became, early in the fourteenth century, the world's chief exporter of quality wool. Production was supervised, and grazing grounds and migration routes controlled, by a powerful ranchers' organization, the Mesta, licensed by Alfonso X in 1273. The export trade created the prosperity of the shipyards and docks of Santander on the north coast, and of Seville in the south. It led to the rapid development of the existing small ports of Castro Urdiales, Laredo and San Vicente de la Barquera, and to the founding of Bilbao in 1300. As a by-product of wool-carrying, Castilian ships also participated in the coastal trade along the Bay of Biscay and western France, carrying cargoes of hides, Toledo arms and English and Flemish cloth. There were Castilian crown representatives in Bruges as early as 1257. During the fourteenth century the Catalan colony was larger than the Castilian, but in the fifteenth century Castilian merchants outnumbered the Catalans in Flanders, and by the early

83 Alfonso X and queen Violante: statue in Burgos cath by a French sculptor c. 1275.

84 A game of chess in a pharmacy: illustration from the *Chess Book of Alfonso the Wise*. Note the medical jars above the players.

fifteenth century Castilian ships were also carrying their hides and wool to Valencia, Majorca and Italy.

The healthy development of the Spanish economy, in both its Aragonese and Castilian phases, was greatly hampered by political instability and by the anti-bourgeois prejudices of the great majority of aristocrats and churchmen. History can only be written on the basis of the available documents, but the historian is often frustratingly aware that the things about which he can write in the most specific and detailed manner are not necessarily those which were the most important. Doctrinal struggles and naked power conflicts within the church can be thoroughly documented, and there is a great deal of information available concerning royal personalities, ambitions and shortcomings. But we know very little about the merchants of Burgos, the shipowners of Santander, the quality arms manufacturers of Toledo, the mercury-miners of Almaden. We also know relatively little about some of the great families whose fortunes were far larger than those of either the Castilian or

Aragonese crown; so that in a certain sense, writing the history of late medieval Spain as the history of kings and their courts is like writing the history of the United States as a series of presidencies, with only scant reference to the roles of the Rockefellers, the Guggenheims, the great railroad and steel magnates. With that unfortunate limitation in mind, we can nevertheless give some indication of the factors which made for instability and civil war, which frustrated economic development and which slowly transformed the pluralistic Spain of Alfonso X and James I into the intolerant Spain of Ferdinand and Isabella.

Both kingdoms had been fortunate in the long reigns of the thirteenth-century reconquest: Ferdinand III (1217–52) and Alfonso X (1252–84) in Castile, and James I (1213–76) in Aragon-Catalonia. Not that these reigns had been at all untroubled. Ferdinand III had had to suppress a revolt in Leon before his sovereign rights were recognized there, and both Alfonso and James faced repeated challenges from the nobility. But for half a century preceding the revolt of Sancho IV against his father Alfonso X, both kingdoms had enjoyed reasonable internal stability and had maintained excellent co-operative relations with each other.

From the late thirteenth century onwards problems of succession were repeatedly to weaken the royal authority in both kingdoms. In 1275 Alfonso's son and heir, Fernando de la Cerda, died on his way to do battle against a Marinid raiding party in Andalusia. According to the strict rule of primogeniture, the latter's infant son then became heir to the throne, and, since the aging Alfonso was unlikely to live for another twenty years, Castile faced the prospect of a regency. Various nobles who resented the centralizing, authoritarian tendencies of Alfonso seized the opportunity to vindicate their own idea of proper Visigothic tradition by 'electing' as heir to the throne the king's younger son Sancho. This action led to eight years of intermittent civil war during which Alfonso 'the Wise' appealed for French intervention on behalf of his grandson (whose

130

85   Sancho IV accompanied by his retinue and the archbishop with his clergy in Toledo cathedral: miniature from an illuminated manuscript of 1285. ▶

mother was Blanche, daughter of saint Louis), was formally deposed by the Cortes in 1282, and spent the last months of his life negotiating for Muslim aid from the Marinids, the very enemy against whom his son Fernando had been preparing to fight at the time of his death. Meanwhile, Sancho was able to pose as the defender of traditional noble prerogatives. After Alfonso's death in 1284, it still took eight years before Sancho was sure of his control of Andalusia; he also had to quell a rebellion among his own supporters who were angered by his employment of a Jew, Abraham de Barchilon (of Barcelona), as principal tax-farmer.

Sancho himself died of tuberculosis in 1296, leaving a nine-year-old son whose capable mother, Maria de Molina, managed to hold the throne for him during five years of civil strife. In the year 1300 this son, now fourteen years of age, was declared to be of age, and mounted the throne as Ferdinand IV. He in turn died in 1312, leaving an infant son. Three mutually hostile nobles, with kingly ambitions of their own, acted as regents until the year 1325, at which time the fifteen-year-old Alfonso XI was declared of age. He was a very energetic, able young man, but not until 1337 could he finally dispose of the repeated revolts raised against him by the ex-regents.

When Alfonso XI died in 1350 he left an official heir, Peter, the son of his Portuguese queen. He had also had twin sons by his mistress, Leonor de Guzman. The legal heir Peter 'the Cruel' (1350–69) apparently connived at the murder of Leonor in 1351, and his entire reign thereafter was filled with civil war between himself and the twin brothers, Henry, count of Trastamara, and Fadrique, master of the order of Santiago. As much by force of circumstances as by personal conviction, Peter now appeared as the champion of centralized, legitimate monarchy. He received the support of that portion of the nobility which favoured the Roman law codes of Alfonso X, and which had approved the efforts of Alfonso XI to put those codes into effect. He also enjoyed the backing of the small Castilian bourgeoisie, and, like his predecessors, he depended upon

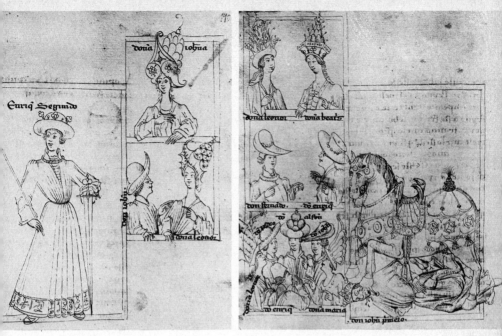

86, 87 Members of the House of Trastamara. Henry IV's court was renowned for fashionable dress and intellectual airs, aptly recorded here by the artist.

Jewish tax-farmers. Henry of Trastamara, like Sancho seventy years earlier, posed as the champion of the decentralizing, Germanic traditions of the Castilian nobility, and appealed also to their anti-semitism, although through his mother Leonor he was himself partly Jewish. England and France intervened in the civil struggle, the former (capriciously and expensively) on behalf of Peter, the latter on behalf of Henry. This particular civil war ended in 1369 when Henry murdered Peter by his own hand.

From 1369 to 1474 Castile was ruled by the Trastamara line. In order to pay their civil-war debts and establish their legitimacy, the first two Trastamara kings, Henry II (1369–79) and John I (1379–90), conceded various portions of the crown income to the nobility. John also made a disastrous attempt to conquer Portugal. Henry III (1390–1406) survived a turbulent minority and during the last years of his short reign managed to recover for the crown some of the tax revenues alienated by his

133

father and grandfather. The reign of John II (1406–54) began with a regency under his astute uncle Ferdinand of Antequera. The king himself was an intelligent, but not a vigorous man. From the age of eight he had been tutored by one Alvaro de Luna, a bastard member of a wealthy *converso* family in Aragon. From the time John was declared of age, in 1419, he depended upon de Luna as the real executive head of the monarchy. The reign was punctuated by civil wars involving shifting alignments of the nobility in both Aragon and Castile; the common denominator of these alignments was the hostility of partisans of de Luna towards those of king John's estranged Trastamara cousins. Don Alvaro triumphed repeatedly, though not easily, until 1453, in which year he was arrested by royal order and executed for witchcraft. The weak king survived by one year the favourite whom he had betrayed under pressure of the anti-*converso* nobility.

John II had been married twice. By his first queen he left a son who reigned as Henry IV (1454–74). By his second queen he left a son, Alfonso, who died in mysterious circumstances at the age of fourteen, and a daughter Isabella, the future queen whose marriage to Ferdinand finally brought about the dynastic union of Castile and Aragon, and whose decisive political ability finally reduced Castile itself to internal order. Henry IV is one of the lesser known and more maligned of Castilian kings. Royal chroniclers performed in the fifteenth century the sort of image-creating which is the province of public relations firms in the twentieth. The royal chroniclers of Queen Isabella, perhaps admiring the lady, but also knowing that their heads might depend upon their interpretations of the 'background' of her reign, effectively blackened the image of Henry IV. He was evidently a large, shambling, awkward man who enjoyed hunting and affected Moorish dress. He understood politics, but did not share the rising anti-Semitic and anti-Muslim feelings of his Castilian subjects. His court was full of Jewish and *converso* intellectuals, some of whom wore long hair and brightly coloured shirts.

Don   enriq·

King Henry IV himself,
in the eccentric dress
r which he was famous.

King Henry also had a Moorish palace guard (as had several
of his predecessors) round which there swirled the usual
rumours of homosexual practices. When Henry's daughter
Juana was born the Cortes accepted her without challenge as his
heir, but several years later the partisans of his younger half-
brother, Alfonso, put about the rumour that the real father of
Juana was not king Henry, but his favourite, Don Beltran de la
Cueva. After all, Henry had been married for six years before
Juana had been born. He consorted with Jews and other long-
hairs, and Don Beltran's rise at court had been mysteriously
rapid. Henry had also offended the more racist of his subjects by
settling a colony of Mudejars near Toledo. The enemies of
Beltran tried to discredit both him and the tolerant king by the
rumour of Juana's illegitimacy. Throughout the 1460s repeated
skirmishes threatened to develop into full civil war, with the
traditionalist, anti-semitic nobility backing Alfonso until his

135

death, and then Isabella; the more pluralistic, bourgeois forces supported king Henry. The latter bought an uneasy peace by agreeing, in the treaty of Toros de Guisando in 1468, to divorce his Portuguese queen, to declare her child Juana illegitimate, and to recognize his half-sister Isabella as heir to the throne. The ensuing marriage of Isabella to her second cousin, Ferdinand, heir to the throne of Aragon, then assured the dynastic union of the kingdoms of Castile and Aragon. The official Isabelline chroniclers, Hernando de Pulgar and Peter Martyr, assiduously emphasized the circumstantial evidence concerning Juana by altering dates and suppressing contrary evidence. The twentieth-century historian Orestes Ferrara has exposed the whole propaganda campaign whereby the child Juana was stigmatized as *la Beltraneja*.

The crown of Aragon suffered similar difficulties with the nobility, with popular prejudice and with royal succession. When James I occupied Valencia and distributed prosperous Muslim farms to his war captains, he created the same sort of rivalry between old and new nobility which plagued his son-in-law Alfonso X in Castile. In 1265 he promised not to create any new nobles in the kingdom of Valencia. His son Peter, by marrying Constance, the daughter of king Manfred of Sicily, extended the dynastic interest in Mediterranean politics. Both Peter III and his son, Alfonso III (1285–91), were to be pre-occupied with the conquests of Sicily and Minorca. The nobles of Aragon took advantage of the foreign-policy problems of their kings to press for political concessions to their own estate. Peter III confirmed the ancient *fueros* of Aragon, and Alfonso III in 1288 had to accept a document forced on him by the union of Aragonese nobles, in which he promised, as king, not to act against any noble without the consent of the Cortes and without confirmation of his action by the *justicia*, an officer whose precise function was to protect the nobility against royal authority. Sixty years later, in 1348, Peter IV (1336–87), at the cost of civil war against both the Valencian and the Aragonese nobility, was able to abolish the concessions made by Alfonso III;

89, 90 Above, king Peter IV of Aragon
Right, king James I of Majorca: the king,
surrounded by laymen and clerics, is being
crowned by two angels. The author,
Romeu des Paol, sits beneath.

but even this imperious, soldierly king had to accept the long-
standing political structure of his dominions whereby Aragon,
Catalonia and Valencia maintained separate Cortes and separate
legal codes.

The course of Mediterranean expansion greatly complicated
the internal dynastic problems of the crown of Aragon. For
most of the time between 1285 and 1374 the Balearic islands and
the province of Roussillon (with its capital at Perpignan)
constituted a separate kingdom of Majorca, ruled by one or
another brother, nephew or cousin of the king of Aragon-
Catalonia. Sicily and Naples were also treated as a dynastic
heritage separate from the realm of Aragon as it had existed
before the late thirteenth-century conquests. In this area the
descendants of James the Conqueror carried on a bitter struggle
with the Angevin dynasty, whose claim to Sicily was backed by
the pope, Martin IV. The pope excommunicated Peter III in a

137

vain effort to prevent Aragonese conquest of Sicily, and throughout the fourteenth century the Aragonese rule of that island was a substantial issue in the complicated politics of the Avignon papacy.

The conquests of Sicily and Sardinia had also left the crown of Aragon with a large number of deserving knights who lacked further bellicose employment. The energies of these men, after 1305, were channelled into several adventures in Greece and Byzantium, and resulted in the conquest of a duchy of Athens which lasted, under the crown of Sicily, from 1326 to 1388. Without going into specific military and political detail one can nevertheless see the complexity of the entire internal power-struggle of the Mediterranean empire of Aragon during the fourteenth century. There were historic, unresolved tensions among the original provinces of Aragon, Catalonia and Valencia. There were efforts to establish and maintain separate crowns of Majorca and Sicily, both of them somehow subsidiary to Aragon and ruled by princes of the house of Aragon. There was war with the Angevin French and the papacy over the control of Sicily, and the costly maintenance of the distant, insecurely held, duchy of Athens. There were, in addition, intermittent naval and piratical engagements with Pisa, Genoa and assorted Muslim naval powers.

In 1410, the death of Martin I without heir brought to an end the dynasty which had supplied Aragon with its kings ever since the marriage of count Ramon Berenguer IV and Petronilla in 1137. The several Cortes could not agree on a single candidate for the vacant throne. One principal contender was the count of Urgel, who was supported by the most powerful family in Aragon, the Lunas, and by the Catalan bourgeoisie. The other leading candidate was Ferdinand of Antequera, a Trastamara and uncle of the boy king John II of Castile. Ferdinand had achieved a high political reputation as regent during John's minority, and a high military reputation for his victory over the Muslims at Antequera. Both the count of Urgel and Ferdinand had approximately equal claims from the standpoint of blood relationship

91, 92   Kings of Aragon. Martin I, from a genealogical table of about 1400, and
Alfonso V the Magnanimous, as portrayed on a contemporary Italian lead medal.

to the late Martin I. But the wealth and political connections of
the Trastamara prince were far greater than those of the count.
Ultimately, Ferdinand was offered the crown of Aragon for
much the same reasons that Henry II of Trastamara had
succeeded in Castile: personal ability, acquisitive energy, the
backing of the conservative small nobility, and the simultaneous
support of a large portion of the *converso* bourgeoisie.

The short reign of Ferdinand of Antequera (1412–16) was a
mixed blessing for Aragon. On the one hand, he contributed
to the final solution of the papal schism, a schism which had
poisoned Aragonese political life for half a century. His coming
also transferred a certain amount of Castilian wealth to Aragon
at a time when the fortunes of Barcelona were vacillating. On
the other hand, he never reconciled the Cortes of Catalonia to his
rule, he devoted his best energies to obtaining high offices and
wealthy marriages for his sons, and he misused for the pacifica-
tion of his new kingdom a large sum of Castilian tax revenues
which had been earmarked for the crusade against the Muslims.
His older son, Alfonso V the Magnanimous (1416–58) invaded

the island of Corsica in 1420 without having made his peace with the three Cortes. He chose to live in Naples, where he became a generous and much-flattered patron of the arts. He left his queen, Maria, to govern Aragon-Catalonia as his regent during the difficult years of Barcelona's economic decline. Meanwhile, his younger brother John, married to queen Blanche of Navarre, ruled that small kingdom and master-minded the campaigns of the Trastamaras of both Castile and Aragon against the Castilian royal favourite, Alvaro de Luna.

At the death of Alfonso V the family holdings were officially divided; Alfonso's bastard son Ferrante inherited the crown of Sicily, and his younger brother John, the crown of Aragon. The family situation of John II of Aragon (1458–79) was also complex. He had had two sons by two wives. The first was Carlos, prince of Viana, who, through his mother queen Blanche, was heir to the thrones of both Navarre and Aragon. His second son was Ferdinand, whose mother was Juana Enriquez, daughter of the powerful and wealthy Fadrique Enriquez, *almirante* of Castile. Ferdinand was always the favoured son, first on grounds of his maternal family connections, and later through his father's recognition of his younger son's superior political ability.

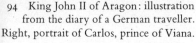

94　King John II of Aragon: illustration
from the diary of a German traveller.
Right, portrait of Carlos, prince of Viana.

John's preference for his younger son, and for Trastamara family interests, led to prolonged and bitter civil war. Under the crown of Aragon it was customary, though not legally binding, for the king to name his eldest son as his 'lieutenant' in Catalonia. In 1460, when John II tried to pass over his elder son Carlos in favour of the eight-year-old Ferdinand, the province rallied, under patriotic and constitutional banners, to the cause of the prince of Viana. The unfortunate prince died in 1461, and John's efforts to install Juana Enriquez, mother of Ferdinand, as governor precipitated a decade of revolution and civil war. The older urban patriciate, supported by a large fraction of the Barcelona artisans and small tradesmen, led the revolt against John; the majority of the prosperous peasants favoured him; the nobility and the clergy were divided. French intervention further weakened the over-all economic and political position of Catalonia, even though, in his eventual victory, John II made statesmanlike concessions to Catalan interests.

141

◀ 93　Friars in attendance at the bier of a king:
from a Book of Ceremonies of the kings of Navarre.

The most striking single characteristic of the Aragonese history just briefly summarized is the sheer dispersal of energy involved: the constitutional and 'estate' rivalries within and between Aragon, Valencia, Catalonia, Roussillon, Sicily, Sardinia, Naples and the Balearics; military adventures in Greece and North Africa; commercial and piratical rivalry everywhere in the Mediterranean; the ups and downs of merchant prosperity in Barcelona, Valencia, Majorca and Naples. The outpouring of energy is comparable with that of the Spaniards in the New World during the sixteenth century. But the Mediterranean empire of the thirteenth, fourteenth and fifteenth centuries was inevitably fragile, not only because of the dynastic divisions, but because the subject peoples could constantly appeal to French or Italian or Muslim interests in order to counterbalance the crown of Aragon.

During these two centuries of economic vitality and political turbulence, the Jews and the Mudejars continued to play much the same roles as they had during the thirteenth century. Both peoples supplied artisans, clothiers, shoemakers, metalworkers to the towns of Castile and Aragon. The Mudejars were especially prominent as skilled farmers, masons and architects. The Jews supplied a high proportion of the tax-collectors, physicians, pharmacists and interpreters. But the fourteenth and fifteenth centuries witnessed a rising tide of anti-semitism, which was clearly related both to the economic growth and the civil wars of the period. All the kings, the great noble families like the Laras and the Haros, the wealthy archbishoprics and the military orders employed Jews as managers of their estates and investments. Certainly the enlightened minority was proud of its tolerant attitude. The great Majorcan scholar and writer Ramon Llull (d. 1315) knew Arabic better than he knew Latin, and was influenced both by the Sufis of Islam and by Maimonides and other Jewish and Arabic philosophers of the Aristotelean tradition. In his *Book of the Gentile and the Three Sages*, representatives of each of three religions, Islam, Judaism and Christianity, expound their beliefs to an intelligent pagan. It is clear

96   Scenes from the life of Ramon Llull. On the left, a Muslim slave teaches Llull Arabic; centre, the Muslim stabs Llull in the stomach; right, Llull finds that the Muslim has hanged himself.

that the author expects the pagan eventually to choose Christianity, but the debate is left incomplete, and no decision is arrived at. D. Juan Manuel, nephew of Alfonso X and one of the regents during the minority of Alfonso XI, referred to his Jewish physician as his one truly intimate, reliable friend. Physicians were frequently also rabbis, and their work was more often like that of modern psychiatrists than physicians. It is thus fully understandable that both their literary culture and their professional practice should make them naturally the confidants of sensitive, wealthy, neurotic patients.

143

But there was a less ideal side to such relationships. Ramon Llull devoted considerable energy to his efforts to convert the Jews of Aragon. His sermons were not as gentle as his philosophical writings, and the real basis of his tolerance was an inner assurance of superiority, and an assumption that conversion would eventually take place. D. Juan Manuel's sentiment concerning his physician might well be duplicated for many an enlightened noble, but what made it possible for such men to 'trust' a Jew was the ferocity of the dynastic struggles and the weakness of the Jews as a numerically small, and by definition inferior, caste.

The most determined enemies of the Jews were the new mendicant orders. In the 1240s Jews and Muslims were ordered by the crown of Aragon to attend the sermons of the Dominicans and Franciscans. Public disputations were organized, in which rabbis debated with friars. Many of these, such as the four-day disputation in Barcelona in 1267, had to be adjourned, despite royal patronage, because of threats of mob violence against rabbis who defended their faith too successfully. Dominican scholars with some knowledge of Hebrew and Aramaic also inspected the available editions of the Talmud and removed therefrom all references to the Messiah. Throughout the two centuries the church pressed the Cortes to pass laws restricting Jewish activities and requiring distinctive Jewish dress. The fact that such legislation had to be repeated indicates that it was no more effective than modern prohibitions against alcohol or marijuana, and it is noteworthy also that the Cortes itself attacked the influence of clerics in government and finance as strongly as it protested against the influence of Jews.

Nevertheless, the general situation of the Jews became increasingly precarious in the fourteenth century. Alfonso XI (1312–50), like his predecessor of the same name, favoured both Jewish administrators and Jewish intellectuals in the early years of his reign. He also used them as scapegoats, and yielded to pressure for forced 'disputations' with friars. In 1348 he announced a new set of laws forbidding Jews and Muslims to

98 Synagogue built by Samuel Halevi shortly before his death.

97 Disputation with the Jews, who are drawn in caricature: from a thirteenth-century manuscript.

lend money at interest or to act as tax-farmers. The laws were modelled on the English legislation of half a century earlier, but whereas the Jews had been officially expelled from England, they were specifically encouraged to stay on in Castile – to buy lands and to engage in commerce, as against lending money. Such laws were a concession both to church pressures and to public opinion as expressed in the Cortes. Yet the need for Jewish administrative services was such that the Cortes of Castile itself asked in 1351 that these laws be revoked.

Alfonso's son, Peter I the Cruel (1350–69), employed Samuel Halevi as his chief tax-collector, member of his privy council alongside two Christian favourites, and ambassador to Portugal. Samuel is famous also as the builder of a beautiful synagogue in his native Toledo. But in 1360 or 1361, for reasons

145

which remain obscure, he was arrested, and taken to Peter's capital, Seville, where he died under torture. His large fortune of gold, silver, lands in the Tagus valley and some eighty Muslim slaves was confiscated by the crown. Some of his relatives, and other important Jewish families, continued to serve the king.

During the civil war between the half-brothers, Henry of Trastamara exploited fully the notion of a royal government mortgaged to the Jews. He collected large ransoms from the Jewish communities of Burgos, Palencia and Toledo at the time of entry to each of those cities. He also used Jews in his own administration, explaining that not enough other qualified civil servants were available, and justifying himself, in comparison with his brother, by assuring the Cortes that there were no Jews on his privy council. On several occasions during the 1360s, English troops intervening on Peter's behalf and French troops serving the cause of Henry perpetrated massacres among the urban Jewish communities.

Probably the largest single factor in the rapid growth of anti-semitism was the ravages of the Black Death. Anywhere from one-quarter to one-half the population of western Europe, including Spain, died of this variety of bubonic plague, which spread rapidly over the Continent in 1348. The sheer massiveness of such mortality entailed a complete breakdown of established authority. Robbery and hysteria became normal occurrences, fields were left uncultivated, shops untended, taxes uncollected. It required a minimum of two years to re-establish normal police, court and notarial services. In the decade following 1348 labour shortages caused wages to quadruple, ruining many a small landlord and at the same time creating a new class of aggressive, rich peasants who profited from the unprecedented opportunity of combining the holdings of their deceased neighbours.

Anti-semitism had been a constant background factor in Europe ever since the first crusade had been preached at the end of the eleventh century. Massacres of Jews had occurred in

Germany, in northern France and in the Near East. On a smaller scale, Jews had also been lynched at tense moments during the reconquest, but on the whole, before 1348, the Jews had suffered less disabilities in Spain than in other parts of western Christendom. The Black Death was now widely attributed to the Jews, and anti-Jewish riots were prominent in the general chaos of the years 1348 to 1351. Lesser outbreaks of the plague occurred in the 1360s and 1370s. Lumping these together with the civil war, the actions of French and English soldiers and the economic depression of 1381, the 'little people' of Spain were ready to blame on the Jews all of their very real, and apparently inexplicable, sufferings.

In the year 1378 Ferrant Martinez, archdeacon of Ecija, began to preach violent sermons against the Jews. He was rebuked by his immediate superior, archbishop Barroso of Seville, but upon the latter's death in 1390 Martinez became the temporary administrator of the diocese of Seville. He called for the razing of all the synagogues in Seville, and urged the peasants to expel the Jews from their villages. The Jewish community appealed for royal intervention, but Castile had just entered upon an uncertain regency following the death of king John I. On 4 June the Jewish quarter was sacked. Some hundreds of Jews were murdered outright, thousands converted rapidly to Christianity, and a large but undetermined number of women and children were sold to Muslim slave traders. About 20 June similar treatment was accorded to the Jewish communities of Cordoba and Toledo. The regency, from Segovia, wrote letters to the city officials of Old Castile, sternly reminding them that the Jews belonged to the king and should be accorded royal protection from mutinous peasants. But the government, whatever its intentions, could not counter the religious fanaticism of the Castilian 'man in the street', and the Jewish quarters of Burgos and other northern towns were also destroyed.

Similar events took place in Aragon, despite the clearly expressed sentiments of king John I and his brother the infante Martin. On 9 July the *aljama* of Valencia was burned by a mob under the leadership of Castilian soldiers awaiting troopships for Sicily. The king by letter rebuked his brother Martin, who was the commander of the forthcoming expedition, but the latter had no control over the mob. Catalonia was proud of a long tradition of toleration, and had in fact received many Jewish refugees from the persecution in southern France during the preceding half century. But early in August some hundred Jews were killed in Barcelona, also by troops awaiting shipment to Sicily. There must have been widespread anti-Jewish feeling among the local populations as well, because the autumn of 1391 witnessed armed attacks and looting of the Jewish quarters in Barbastro, Lerida and Jaca. When the count of Ampurias sheltered the Jews of Gerona in his castle at Geronella, the local peasants besieged the castle. The prestige of the monarchy prevented fatal riots in the capital city of Saragossa, and damage was limited in Tarragona, seat of the oldest archbishopric in the realms of Aragon. The crown tried to react vigorously, not only because the Jews were valuable to it, but also because the riots involved elements of general social protest as well as anti-semitism. A handful of mob leaders was executed in several cities, but in general, during 1392, the restoration of order was accompanied by a whitewash of the rioters.

A pronounced tendency developed during the fourteenth century for intellectual and aristocratic Jews to convert to Christianity. The documentary evidence is too thin to form the basis for generalizations, and understandably there have been strong emotions on the part of both Jewish and Christian scholars writing on the subject. But it is clear that such tendencies were present independent of catastrophic events such as the Black Death or the pogroms of 1391, and that the early conversions among intellectuals were truly voluntary. In the halcyon days of Alfonso X, 'King of the Three Religions' in the mid thirteenth century, it had seemed that an era of complete toleration and symbiosis among the three communities might be dawning. Jewish translators and civil servants were deeply grateful to the king, and were of course influenced by a Christian environment in which they were not treated as outcasts. Many deeply religious spirits rejected the exclusiveness of Jewish claims to be the Chosen People. They felt the challenge of Christian thought to the whole notion of the Messiah. They might learn to prefer Christian theology to either the tortuously legalistic Talmud, or the cool rationalism of Maimonides.

One such intellectual, neither a wealthy nor a politically prominent man, was Abner of Burgos, later known by his Christian name as Master Alfonso of Valladolid. Abner had apparently had dreams and nightmares over a period of twenty-five years, dreams in which he felt urgently called upon to convert. In 1320 he announced his conversion in a book entitled *The Wars of the Lord*, which has been preserved only in part. The surviving portions breathe hatred of the Talmud and of Maimonides. They laud the determinism and the predestination of Paul and Augustine. They admire the ardent flame of medieval Christian mysticism. Defending himself against the attacks of his former co-religionists, Alfonso pointed to the example of Abraham, who had found his new faith and left his home at the age of fifty-two.

Seventy years later another native of Burgos, this time a scion of an old and wealthy tax-farming family, left the Jewish community. Solomon Halevi, aged forty, serving Castile as a diplomat in France, decided sometime in either 1390 or 1391 to become a Christian, and returned to Burgos to be baptized under the name Paul of Santa Maria. Returning to Paris in order to study theology, he became a friend of cardinal Pedro de Luna, who in 1394 became pope Benedict XIII. Paul preached antisemitic sermons in Avignon and tried unsuccessfully to get king John I of Aragon to enact restrictive laws in his realms. From 1396 he was a canon of the cathedral in Burgos, and later became chaplain to king Henry III. Upon the latter's death he served in the regency of the boy king John II, and in 1415 he became bishop of Burgos.

Paul of Santa Maria is a dramatic, but by no means rare, example of a Jewish convert who became a powerful and zealous persecutor of the Jews. He co-operated actively in the efforts of saint Vincent Ferrer to eliminate the Jewish communities of Castile. During the first years of the regency, Ferrer toured the cities of Castile, exhorting the Jews voluntarily to convert. At the same time, he and his peasant followers terrorized the Jews by entering synagogues and proclaiming their conversion to use as churches, and by evicting Jews from their homes whenever they had the misfortune to own property in the centre of Christian towns or neighbourhoods. He urged on the crown a new set of restrictive laws which were enacted in 1412. Jews were to be forbidden to serve as tax-farmers or other government officials. The remaining communities (those which had escaped destruction in 1391) were to lose their traditional independent municipal status. Friar Vincent, strongly supported by bishop Paul, wished to establish a true *apartheid*. Jews were to grow their hair long, wear beards and distinctive dress. They were to be confined to specific residential areas, and Jewish doctors, merchants and artisans were not to serve Christian clients. As in the past, such laws could not be completely observed, but this time they had the sanction of the royal government and the support of a highly prestigious *converso*.

Meanwhile, in Aragon, king Martin I had died in 1410, and after a two-year interregnum, the crown had been offered to Ferdinand of Antequera. Ferdinand had governed Castile from 1406 to 1410 as regent for his nephew, the young John II. To a considerable degree he owed his election in Aragon to the strong support of Vincent Ferrer. The latter was as anxious to convert the Jews of Aragon as he was to convert the Jews of Castile. He was a highly influential figure at the court of Benedict XIII, who, as the 'anti-pope' in the schism of the Roman church, had taken up residence in Tortosa. As a member of a *converso* family, and as a 'pope' who had fled for his life from Avignon, and who was recognized neither in Italy nor in France, Benedict was especially anxious to prove both his personal authority and his orthodox Christianity. In addition, he was a strong proponent of the tradition of Roman law in Spain, and that tradition em-

The profession of Saint Vincent: detail from a fifteenth-century altarpiece.

phasized the importance of single, centralized authority in both secular and religious affairs. Saint Vincent Ferrer and pope Benedict counted on each other's support for a campaign to convert the Jews. They assumed also that they would receive the backing of Ferdinand of Antequera, who owed to them his elevation to the throne of Aragon.

The personal physician of Benedict XIII was a Jew named Joshua Halorki. In the year 1412 Ferrer persuaded him to convert. Taking the name Hieronymus of the Holy Faith, Dr Halorki hastily put together an anthology of Jewish writings, some of them forgeries, which pointed to the acceptance of Christ as the Messiah. In November 1412, Benedict solemnly invited the Jewish communities of Aragon each to send a deputation of scholars to the papal court at Tortosa, for the purpose of taking part in a 'debate' which would prove conclusively the truth of Christianity as against Judaism. The proceedings opened in January 1413 before an assemblage of red-robed cardinals. Dr Halorki announced that his proof would be based upon the following syllogism, illustrated abundantly by citations from the Talmud: The Man in whom prophecies are fulfilled is the Messiah; the prophecies were fulfilled in Jesus; therefore Jesus is the Messiah. The debate continued at intervals for a full year. The early sessions were conducted by oral argument, the later ones in the form of written depositions. The Jews were completely on the defensive from the start, and in April the papal representatives introduced forced, and possibly forged, testimony, to the effect that a number of Jewish scholars had admitted that the Messiah had indeed already appeared. Meanwhile, Vincent Ferrer was fulminating in the synagogues of Aragonese towns and King Ferdinand, embarrassed by his zeal and by the violence of his followers, tried to get him to preach in Tortosa and Saragossa, where the more sophisticated urban communities might dampen the melodramatic effects of his speeches.

In part, the Jews prolonged the debate in the hope that Ferdinand might intervene on their behalf. Much as he owed his throne to Benedict, he must surely be concerned for the prosperity of his kingdom, and for the fact that the church everywhere but in Spain was preparing to end the schism by recognizing the Roman pontiff. Ferdinand was indeed negotiating with the Jews, and by early in the year 1414 D. Vidal ben Benevist de la Cavalleria, the most brilliant of the Jewish delegates, had become a Christian and had re-entered the service of the royal treasury under the name of D. Gonzalo de la Cavalleria. The Disputation of Tortosa was officially terminated in 1415 with the publication of a set of anti-Jewish laws paralleling those of 1412 in Castile.

The next year the political situation changed with a change of key personalities. The tolerant, cultured Alfonso V succeeded his father Ferdinand in Aragon. John II was declared major in Castile, and developed into a king who patronized culture and deplored fanaticism. The new Roman pope, Martin V, was also a mild, tolerant man, and by the action of these three, most of the laws advocated by Vincent Ferrer were suspended. But urban public opinion opposed this suspension, and in any case the morale of the Jewish communities in both kingdoms had been virtually destroyed by the pogroms of 1391 and the events of 1412 to 1416.

The mass conversions among Jews at the end of the fourteenth century produced an entirely new social group which had no specific legal status and no spiritual cohesion, the so-called *conversos* or New Christians. A few conversions resulted from genuine intellectual and religious changes of outlook. A larger number represented frank and sceptical accommodation to an apparent situation of fact: anti-Jewish feeling was rising steadily in Spain, but the Jews could save not only their lives, but their livelihood and their broad cultural role if they were willing to become Christians. The majority of conversions, especially among the artisans and small merchants, were motivated by simple visceral fear. In point of fact, throughout the fifteenth century, *conversos* performed the same services to Spanish society as had the Jews in previous centuries. The crown, the aristocracy and the upper bourgeoisie gladly welcomed this apparent solution of the Jewish problem. The great *converso* families, the Lunas, the Mendozas, the Guzmans, the Enriquez, filled the high offices of church and state. There were even literary satires and much good-humoured joking about the Jewish blood in the veins of every important family in the realm. The Trastamara family was descended from the Jewish mistress of Alfonso XI, and the mother of the prince Ferdinand who married Isabella was a *converso*, Juana Enriquez.

But mass conversion did not eliminate the ethnic prejudices of the Old Christians of Castile, and it split the former Jewish community into two mutually fearful and scornful camps. The Jewish 'establishment', the rabbis and notaries and *aljama* officers, had always frowned upon intermarriage. Now they increasingly employed informers to trace the lineage, the social and business connections, of their fellow Jews. At the same time some *conversos* became zealous persecutors of their former co-religionists, while others hoped that rational, sceptical, and simply humane considerations would heal the wounds and allow them to play a constructive intermediary role between the Christian and Jewish communities.

The quantitative importance of conversion and intermarriage produced a new concern with *limpieza de sangre*, purity of blood. This question had been very important to the ruling aristocracy of Muslim Spain under the emirs and caliphs, and the revolt of anti-Arab ethnic groups had been a major ingredient in the break-up of the caliphate. Similarly, purity of blood was to become an important political criterion in Spain of the late fifteenth to the seventeenth century. But throughout the central period of the Middle Ages, very few persons outside the church and the rabbinate had been concerned about intermarriage. When the notion of blood purity as a qualification for office emerged again in the mid-fifteenth century, it was decisively rejected by both the royal government and the church. But gradually, between 1467 and 1547, it was accepted by various orders and cathedral chapters, and it became one of the curses of Spanish society in the sixteenth and seventeenth centuries. Meanwhile, from 1391 onwards, the decimated Jewish communities and the new caste of *conversos* lived between opportunism and terror.

100 Carved capitals in Barcelona cathedral show a group of Jews with the distinctive badge they were compelled to wear by order of the third and fourth Lateran Councils.

V LITERATURE AND PAINTING
IN MEDIEVAL SPAIN

It will already be clear to any reader of the present work that medieval Spain enjoyed a vigorous intellectual and artistic life. During the centuries of Muslim dominion important works of theology, law, astronomy, botany and mathematics had been produced. Translation of Persian, Hindu and Greek manuscripts had enriched the Arabic cultural heritage and testified to the eclecticism, tolerance and absorptive capacity of Muslim culture. Al-Andalus had produced highly refined lyric poetry in Arabic, and popular poetry in both Arabic and Romance. Significantly, for comparison with later Castilian and Catalan literature, it had not produced drama with realistic, credibly differentiated and individualized characters. Muslim Spain had also developed extraordinary craft traditions in the working of metals, leather, textiles, ivory, wood and ceramics; and it had evolved architectural forms which were at once spacious, dignified, aesthetically pleasing and well integrated into the natural landscape. The fine artisan and architectural traditions had all been transmitted to Christian Spain through Mozarabic and Mudejar craftsmen, and were widely practised from the twelfth century onwards by Christian artisans in northern Spain. The scientific and philosophical books became known in the late thirteenth century thanks to the efforts of Alfonso X and his translator-scholars. The influence of Arabic and early Romance poetry made itself felt more in the realm of folk-songs and 'minstrel shows' than in the form of translation and scholarship. The architecture, the sculpture and the decorative styles of the later Middle Ages represented a wonderfully flexible synthesis of the Romanesque, the Cistercian Gothic and the Mudejar.

It remains for us to trace the beginnings of poetry in the Romance languages, and of painting, two forms of art which

155

101, 102 The tradition of oral culture. Left, twelfth-century carving of minstrels in the monastery of Santa Maria de L'Estany. Right, a page from the first written version of *The Cid*, set down nearly two centuries after its original composition.

date from the early twelfth century and which have been practised vigorously in Spain ever since. The first major literary work in Castilian which has come down to us is the *Poem of the Cid*. The poem deals with the career of a heroic minor noble who, as we have seen (above pp. 60–65), had served, and later been exiled by, king Alfonso VI, and who had briefly conquered Valencia from the Almoravids in 1094. There are enough other documentary references to the Cid to make it certain that, in contrast with the heroes of the Norse legends or the *Song of Roland*, he is indeed a historically identifiable personage. The poem may be described succinctly as a novelized biography. The references to the Cid's political and military methods, and to his relations with Alfonso VI, are largely historical. The account of his relations with his subordinates, with his wife and with the Cluniac bishop Jerome, whom he invited to Valencia, are highly credible if not directly verifiable. The story of the first disastrous marriages of his two daughters is probably legendary, but is also probably as close to the poetic truth as are many of the incidents in contemporary novels and films based on the lives of historical figures.

In any case, the spirit of the poem is far more important than the degree of its literal truthfulness. Composed in about 1140, approximately forty years after the death of the Cid himself, it tells a great success story, starting with the undeserved exile of the Cid and his swindling of two Jewish money-lenders, and ending in his full reconciliation with Alfonso VI, and the marriage of his daughters to princes of Navarre and Aragon. At all times the poet emphasizes his energy, his military prowess, his charisma as felt both by his soldiers and by his conquered subjects. He portrays the Cid as generous and warm-hearted to his family and followers, and as overflowing with humour and gusto. The poet has a strong juridical sense, and emphasizes the

Cid's obedience to his sovereign despite the injustices he has allegedly suffered. He is shown as morally superior to the hereditary nobility, and as thoroughly enjoying every challenge which life offers him. He engages in complex alliances and negotiations, but has no Hamlet-like hesitations and always has a good conscience concerning his own acts and those of his friends. While frankly seeking conquest and wealth, he has no doubt that his personal cause coincides with justice and the will of God. His rational and legal calculations, however, have to do with war, economics and social position, not with theology or with crusades against the infidel. Altogether this intelligent, courageous, successful minor nobleman is the great folk-hero of the people of Castile, that people which occupied a rude frontier, which had to expand or die, and which had to assert itself politically against both Islam and the traditional prestige of the older Christian kingdom of Leon.

But the *Poem of the Cid* has never been read solely for its subject-matter and the symbolic significance of its hero. It is a marvel of dramatic energy, beautiful both in literary quality and in sheer sound. The descriptive phrases simultaneously characterize the individuals and pace the narrative. The verse is rhythmically variable, with anything from eleven to seventeen feet in a line. Both a strong and a weak accent in each half-line make for effective oral presentation, and in most cases help to emphasize meaning. Assonance lends a musical quality, while the irregular length of line avoids any danger of a sing-song pattern. Speeches as well as descriptions are both brief and dramatic. Although the poem was composed in 1140, the oldest copy of it in existence dates from 1307. Thus the beauty, the simplicity, the rhythm and accent of the language owe something to the popular oral traditions through which it was preserved during more than a century and a half. *The Cid*, then, inaugurates a tradition of intimate spontaneous collaboration between professional writers and the common people, a tradition which became a major ingredient of both the drama of the Golden Age and the fiction and poetry of modern times.

Dating from almost a century later than *The Cid* is the work of the first great lyric poet in the Castilian language, Gonzalo de Berceo (*c.* 1200–65). Berceo was a monk, and spent his entire life within a few miles of the monastery of San Millan de la Cogolla. Nestling high in the foothills of La Rioja, the monastery of San Millan looks out upon a truly smiling landscape: temperate, well watered, with alternating grain-fields, orchards and evergreen forests. It lies fairly close to the pilgrimage route to Santiago, and the poet must have had frequent opportunities to talk with foreigners and to hear news of the outside world. It should be noted as well that he lived during the decades of the triumphant reconquest of Andalusia and the Levant, that he was a contemporary of Ferdinand III, of James I (the Conqueror) of Aragon, of Alfonso X (the Wise) of Castile, of saint Louis and of Thomas Aquinas. A quiet life, then, in a beautiful geographical setting, punctuated by conversation concerning great events and great thoughts.

Berceo specialized in verse translation from the Latin original. He thought of himself as a *juglar*, a professional composer and reciter for a large audience, but his subject-matter was the lives of saints, rather than the deeds of secular or legendary heroes. His *Life of St Domingo* is taken word for word from a Latin biography dating from 1090. That of San Millan likewise is based upon Latin documents, to which he adds his personal knowledge of the local landscape and history. He is at the same time matter-of-fact concerning his own limitations as a Latinist. He wrote in a carefully measured verse, known as *mester de clerecia*, since it was created and used by priestly poets. It consisted of four-line stanzas, with thirteen to fifteen syllables in a line, two heavy and two light accents per line, and a single rhyme for each stanza. It was meant to be recited rather than sung, and in the hands of Berceo it is a much calmer, less dramatic, form of verse than that found in *The Cid*. Critics often find him monotonous, and certainly most of his language and imagery is quite conventional. I find his verbal music completely charming, but it is a charm comparable with that of the early

Mozart, rather than with that of Beethoven or Wagner. He wrote simultaneously to entertain and to instruct. He wanted to be understood by ordinary folk. There is a candid, natural, easy-going tone to all his description and narration. His humour prompts a quiet smile more than a belly laugh. He is decorous without affectation. There are also moments of high poetic rapture, and he sets an example, which has inspired many later Spanish poets, of the successful fusion of the mundane and popular with the mystically ecstatic.

Thus by the mid-thirteenth century both epic and didactic narrative poetry were being written in Castilian, and the work of Berceo was well known and appreciated within his own lifetime. But the first 'romantic', personally lyrical poetry we know of in Christian Spain was composed in the Galician-Portuguese language. The Galician lyric flourished from the late twelfth to the mid-fourteenth century, and some two thousand examples of it have survived. The notion of love as a proper subject-matter for poetry entered Spain in the person of Provençal poets who travelled along the pilgrimage route to Santiago, and who resided at the court of the Burgundian prince Henry, founder of the kingdom of Portugal. The Provençal troubadours addressed their verses both to inaccessible great ladies and to naïve country lasses. In the more highly sophisticated society of France, poems of Platonic love dedicated to noble ladies were more common. In the simpler society of north-western Spain the lyrics were dedicated proportionately more often to shepherdesses and village belles. A special class of love poems distinctive to Galicia were the *cantigas de amigo*, love poems sung by girls about their suitors, or absent or lost lovers. These poems celebrate the love of nature, and the love of women for men. They are particularly sensitive to youthful emotions, to the uncertainty and insecurity of adolescent, newly awakened feelings. They are bathed in an atmosphere of gentle, often narcissistic, melancholy – an ambience summed up in the word *saudade*, which still retains a key role in the entire poetic and musical culture of the Portuguese and Brazilian people.

103   Dancing figures decorate an early fourteenth-century bowl.

These Galician love poems were composed in two basic forms: the *zejel* and the *cossante*. The *zejel* was a Spanish-Arabic creation consisting of two or three very short line stanzas connected by a one- or two-line refrain. It had been danced and sung in the streets of al-Andalus. Many of the *zejels* were bilingual, and it is probable that most of the northern Christians who heard them did not understand either the Arabic or the Romance vocabulary in which they were composed. But they could easily have acquired a feeling for the art form, just as many Americans learn to appreciate Italian opera without ever knowing a word of Italian. The *cossante* was a music and dance form probably of pagan origin. The lines were longer than those of

161

the *zejel*, and were bound together more by assonance than by rhyme. A special feature of the *cossante* text was the constant near-repetition of the lines, and the slight rearrangement of key phrases from verse to verse. The two forms offered much greater flexibility of both vocabulary and rhythm than did the *mester de clerecia* in Castilian. There may also have been subconscious political and psychological reasons why, in the thirteenth century, Castilian seemed to be a proper vehicle for learned prose, for religious or epic poetry, but not for the softer emotions of love. In any case, the first body of medieval Spanish love poetry was composed in Galician, and not until the fifteenth century were these flexible forms and lyric emotions assimilated into Castilian.

The first great master of secular, stylistically varied Castilian poetry was Juan Ruiz, archpriest of Hita (*c.* 1280–*c.* 1350). In the perspective of such later events as the inquisition and the counter-reformation, it is a delightful irony that Juan Ruiz should have been a priest, and this should also be borne in mind by anyone wishing to understand the truly ecumenical and humane spirit of medieval Spanish culture at its best. The archpriest made his home some thirty miles east of Alcala de Henares, in the centre of the Castilian *meseta*, and within easy reach of the royal city of Segovia. He is known to us through one great book, the *Libro de Buen Amor*, the *Book of the Good Love* (or *Fellowship*), a collection of narrative and lyric poems held together by a quasi-autobiographical thread. Much ink has been spilled over the question whether the archpriest actually experienced all the sexual adventures of which he writes in the first person singular. In all likelihood his book is novelized autobiography, much as *The Cid* is novelized biography. He must have had some such experiences as he describes. The tone is too earthily realistic to reflect merely second-hand experience. But as a priest he would have heard many confessions that would add to his stock of available material, and medieval audiences were accustomed to hear minstrels sing in the first person of adventures which were not literally their own.

104 The marques de Santillana kneeling in prayer. Book collector and commentator on Romance literatures, the marques is especially remembered for his delightful and earthy *serranillas*.

Juan Ruiz wrote his narratives in the same verse form as Berceo had used: four-line stanzas averaging fourteen syllables to the line, with a single rhyme for each stanza. But this form, known as *mester de clerecia* when employed by priests, was in its wider secular use called *cuaderna via*. The poet also wrote hymns in lines of eight syllables, with varied rhyme schemes; racy *zejels* in the Spanish-Arabic tradition; and *serranillas*, short, humorous lyrics in six- and seven-syllable lines, about encounters in the mountain wilderness with shepherdesses of strong and varied temperaments. The remarkable common denominator in his handling of all verse forms is the immediate conversational intonation that he achieves within each poetic convention. And while metrically his *cuaderna via* is precisely the same as Berceo's metre, his actual tempi are much more varied and supple.

Just as his forms are miscellaneous, so are his subjects: love adventures among all social classes; conversations with students, beggars, minstrels, travellers of all kinds. His emotional attitude seems to me especially Spanish. Life is full of drama, conflict and disappointment. All the peripeteia of fate are met energetically. 163

Real misfortune is accepted stoically; failures in the pursuit of the fair sex are treated ironically, but still with respect for strong human feelings. These realistic attitudes, and the swift dramatic expression of feeling, avoid the kind of brooding, internalized resentment which brings modern man to the psychiatrist's couch. At the same time, it is difficult to gauge the extent of the archpriest's influence. His work was known to the marques de Santillana and a few other fifteenth-century poets, but he was not widely read in Spain until the mid-nineteenth century. His verve, his knowledge of and affection for the common people, his bubbling humour and his earthiness all remind one of both Cervantes and Galdos, in short, of those supreme prose masters who have portrayed the inner life of the Spanish people.

Very different in spirit from the archpriest was his contemporary D. Santob de Carrion (*fl.* 1340s). D. Santob wrote in both Hebrew and Castilian, and was a public opponent of the recently converted Jew, Abner of Burgos. He dedicated his lyrics to prince Peter, the future king Peter the Cruel, who was considered, with some justice, to be amicably disposed towards the Jewish community. D. Santob celebrated the beauty of nature with the same fervour as did the Galician poets, but without the need for narrative as the occasion for such expression. He wrote sensuous love lyrics, more tender and melancholy than those of Juan Ruiz, and again perhaps reminiscent of the Galician style. More particularly, he is the first Castilian poet to write specifically in praise of books, of philosophical instruction and conversation. As a Spanish Jew writing in the fourteenth century, his intellectual horizon stretched from Burgos through Andalusia, across North Africa to the Middle East. It barely noticed the medieval Latin world. While this fact is particularly evident in D. Santob, it may be said generally that during the fourteenth century the thought and literature of Christian Spain were still more deeply influenced by the Islamic heritage than by the western European. Thus both Ramon Llull and Juan Ruiz show more Arabic than Latin influences in their style and outlook.

A final major element in medieval Castilian poetry is the *romances*, the first examples of which date from the period of the civil war of the 1360s, between Peter the Cruel and his half-brother Henry of Trastamara. These were ballads of varying length, composed of eight-syllable lines connected by assonance, and meant to be sung. They appear to have been the product of village rather than city or court, and were the work of individual poets, but were spontaneously revised in the course of oral transmission. Thus, like *The Cid*, they represent the fusion of conscious craftsmanship with anonymous popular expression. They deal with warfare, and with the effects of war on those who remain at home or are victimized by the passage of troops. They are realistic, starkly dramatic, free of complex metaphors. They can be sympathetic to a defeated enemy (often a Muslim), show no religious or ethnic prejudices, and usually contain no moral judgments on the events described. As in *The Cid* or in Juan Ruiz, life is essentially a series of dramatic encounters. To live well is to feel things deeply, and to act energetically, whatever the cause, win or lose. The *romance* flourished from the 1360s until the reign of Ferdinand and Isabella, and reflects directly the vitality, the candour, and the broad sympathies of the Spanish people.

The best of medieval Catalan literature was written in prose: the philosophical works by Ramon Llull and the chronicles of Mediterranean expansion by Ramon Muntaner. Possibly the influences of Provence and Languedoc in the High Middle Ages, and of Italy in the fifteenth century, made it difficult for the Catalans to create a distinctive poetic language. The one poet, at least among those whose work is now known, who compares qualitatively with a Gonzalo de Berceo or a Juan Ruiz, is the fifteenth-century poet Auzias March (1397–1459). March was a courtier who apparently 'went too far' in an illicit love-affair, was therefore exiled from royal service in 1429, and spent the remaining thirty years of his life on his extensive private estate hawking, making love and writing. His poetry is distinguished, somewhat like that of John Donne, by an im-

105 Hawking: detail from the altarpiece of St Bartholomew, school of Tarragona.

106 Manuscript page of the poetry of Auzias March.

mense intellectual effort to capture all the exquisite and tortured nuances of his inner life. He was preoccupied with death, with guilt-feelings about sensual love, and with uncertainty about the real nature of his emotions. His poetry is a philosophical effort to make his complex feelings intelligible. His metaphors are long and complicated, and his entire style stands in marked contrast with the direct, exuberant, life-loving tone of the Castilian poetry discussed above.

While the leading poets of the Spanish Middle Ages were clearly Galician or Castilian, the great painters were most frequently Catalans, Valencians or Andalusians working in the kingdom of Aragon-Catalonia. Spanish medieval painting begins with the frescoes painted on the walls of the apses of Romanesque churches in the Catalan Pyrenees. In themes and iconography they are clearly descended from the Byzantine

166

107 Santa Maria de Esterri d'Aneu. Fresco from the main apse, showing a seraph and the prophet Elijah.

108 The bulls of Tahull,
predecessors of those
painted by Picasso:
detail from the apse
fresco of San Clemente
de Tahull.

109 The Christ Pantoc
surrounded by four a
dominates the same cl
In his left hand he
the text, 'I am the
of the w

mosaics. But fresco, the laying of colours on wet plaster, was at once a swifter, cheaper and more flexible way of decorating a large surface. The work was probably done in two stages: the broad background was painted in strips of solid, bright colours such as yellow, ochre, red and blue; afterwards, on a second thin layer of plaster, the artist would add line-drawing and decorative detail. The speed of the fresco technique made it easier for the individual artist to express his personal vision.

Artistically the most impressive of the Catalan Romanesque frescoes are those of San Clemente de Tahull, probably completed in the year 1123, and transferred early in the present century to the museum of Catalan Art in Barcelona. They are outstanding for their careful architectural use of the curved walls and dome, for their firm over-all design, for the sumptuous draping of the human figures, for the strong colours, and for the

168

life-like, energetic, penetrating gaze of the Christ Pantocrator. We do not know how much the art of twelfth-century Catalonia may have been influenced by Islamic models just to the south. Since the Muslims, like the Jews, imposed a religious prohibition against the representation of the Godhead, their decorative art in the mosques was entirely abstract. In their ceramics and textiles, however, they drew birds and animals in a wide variety of the most naturalistic and fantastic styles. In the Tahull frescoes the recognizable although distorted bulls may well owe something to the art of Spanish Islam, and in any event they are evidently the ancestors of the tortured bulls painted by Picasso in his *Guernica* mural.

A striking characteristic of most of the twelfth-century Catalan murals is the relative complexity of the background details: the geometrical wainscoting below the band of printed words, and the botanical and animal themes in the decoration of the columns, or in the oval enclosing the figure of the Pantocrator. The decoration of mosques and Islamic palaces was characterized particularly by the use of detailed design covering the entire surface, and this feature of Islamic art may well have influenced the Catalan fresco-painters. The total impression made by the Tahull frescoes is one of creative imagination, energy, grandeur of design, technical mastery of the medium, and openness to the full range of Byzantine, French and Hispano-Arab precedents. During the twelfth and thirteenth centuries many churches in Aragon, and even as far west as Berlanga de Duero in Old Castile, were decorated with similar frescoes. But generally speaking there was no significant advance in the technique of such painting, and nothing has survived which is superior, or even equal to, the Tahull paintings of 1123. (See map p. 127.)

The next important advance in Spanish painting occurred in the work of Ferrer Bassa (*c.* 1285–1348). Bassa must have been an impressive personality. His long career included a death sentence for criminal assault in 1315, several pardons by king James II of Aragon, and diplomatic missions for king Peter IV,

110 Ferrer Bassa, *The Adoration of the Magi* (1345–46), from the murals in the convent of the Nuns of St Clare.

who appointed him court painter. His only surviving work is a set of murals in the convent of the Nuns of St Clare, in Pedralbes, near Barcelona. These murals were done in oil-paints rather than fresco. They are the earliest known examples of such treatment of wall surfaces, and Bassa seems to have employed a thus far unidentified ingredient which greatly retarded the normal cracking and fading of oils. The murals picture scenes

171

from the life of Christ. His representation of figures, and his ability to convey a sense of volume and weight, may owe something to the influence of Giotto, but his facial expressions, his decorative ability with garments and drapes, and his suggestiveness without literal detail (most evident in the *Adoration of the Magi*) show his marked originality.

Contemporary with, and later than, Ferrer Bassa are numerous interesting murals and also oil-painted altarpieces in the Gothic churches built in the fourteenth century. Italian influence, particularly that of the Sienese school, spread rapidly in the second half of the century, and was successfully assimilated by competent but not highly original painters such as the brothers Jaume and Pedro Serra, and Luis Borrassa. During the

172

112 Luis Borrassa, *St Peter Walking on the Water* (1411).

113   *Nativity* (1475), by the Master of Avila.

fifteenth century Flemish influence dominated painting in both
Aragon and Castile. Luis Dalmau (d. 1463) travelled to Bruges
to study under Jan Van Eyck in 1431. King John II of Castile
was an enthusiastic and knowledgeable art patron, one of
whose favourite painters was Roger van der Weyden; and
Jaime Huguet, the leading Catalan painter of the later fifteenth
century, was in many respects a disciple of van der Weyden.
Both Italian and Flemish artists were commissioned to decorate
the cathedrals of Toledo and Leon, and the palaces of the great
nobles of Castile. Their native peers, such as the Master of
Sopetran, the Master of Avila and Fernando Gallego, all
painted in styles which show a predominantly Flemish influence.

The *Devout before the Tomb of* *[V]incent*, attributed to Jaime Huguet. [A v]ariety of votive images hang above [the] body of the saint.

The influence of Flanders is parti-
[cular]ly notable in a detail of the *Virgin* [of th]e *Councillors*, attributed to Luis
[D]au (below).

[Far] Right, Fernando Gallego (c. 1440–
[   ], *Christ in Majesty*.

117 Bartolome Bermejo, *Pietà*.

The outstanding individual artist of the fifteenth century was Bartolome Bermejo (d. 1498), who was of Andalusian origin and who did his major work for Catalan patrons. In 1490, commissioned by canon Luis Despla, he executed a magnificent *Pietà* in the cathedral of Barcelona. In the foreground, an austerely grieving Mary holds the rigid corpse of her crucified Son. A troubled, but still self-controlled, St Dominic observes

118 *The Arrest of Santa Engracia*, also by Bartolome Bermejo.

from one side while reading a holy text. On the other kneels canon Despla, unshaven, gazing in sleepless sorrow at the dead Christ. Behind St Dominic lies a brooding, stormy landscape with a delicately modelled, and highlighted, palace and windmill. Behind canon Despla rises a Gothic city, and in the doorway of a stone house sits a peasant woman, quietly surveying the scene of Calvary. The whole painting has the architectural grandeur and the rich decorative detail which grew out of the centuries-old Hispano-Arab tradition, and which was to reach perfection in the work of El Greco. It has the intensity of emotional expression, the dramatic quality, the brooding religious preoccupation which were characteristic of Spain at the end of the Middle Ages and which were carried forward into the art and literature of the Golden Age.

Indeed, it is essential to recognize the continuity and the open-endedness of the development of literature and painting in the Spanish Middle Ages. Geopolitically and institutionally, the era from 711 to 1492, from the Arab invasion to the end of the reconquest and the discovery of America, can be treated logically as a unit. But for art and literature, the logical unit would be rather the period from about 1100 to 1700. At the earlier date one sees Christian Spain beginning to assimilate the arts and the architecture of al-Andalus, and the beginnings of literature in a language which is recognizably the direct ancestor of modern Castilian. With the composition of *The Cid*, and with the Catalan frescoes, one sees the strong beginning of native traditions in literature and painting. For six centuries thereafter, Spanish culture constantly exhibits the artisan traditions, the skill with a wide variety of materials, the preoccupation with architecture and over-all decoration, the Arabic and Hebrew intellectual influences, the tension between orthodoxy and heterodoxy, between authoritarianism and pluralism, and the symbiosis between the consciously artistic and the popular: in short, all those traits which form the common denominator of, and give their peculiar stamp to, what we know as classic Spanish art and literature.

In the eyes of any politically conscious Spaniard living in 1460 the future of both the Castilian and Aragonese monarchies must have appeared precarious. Resentment against Jews and *conversos*, against Genoese bankers and Catalan merchants, was but one aspect of the large movements of social protest occurring in the fifteenth century. In Galicia, Aragon and Majorca there were important peasant and urban lower-class revolts during the 1460s. We do not yet have detailed studies of these movements, but they all involved a clash between clerical and noble landlord interests and a 'revolution of rising expectations', based upon the demographic and economic advances which were vaguely sensed, if not clearly understood, by all classes of the population.

One such struggle, carefully studied by Spain's greatest historian of the twentieth century, the late Jaime Vicens Vives, was that of the *payeses de remensa* in Catalonia. The *remensa* was the money price which peasants had been required to pay to their hereditary landlords for permission to leave the land. It had been designed in part to slow down the emigration of peasants to the city. By the mid-fifteenth century it was hated as the symbol of all the numerous taxes through which the landed nobility exploited the peasantry. At the same time, because of rising prices and pretensions as to standard of living, the nobles collected all the taxes more vigorously than in previous centuries. The peasants were acutely conscious not only of the actual increase in their money payments, but also of the humiliation involved in having legally to buy their right to emigrate from the farms. Both Alfonso V and John II had tended to support their demand for the abolition of the *remensa*, but the urban patriciate of Barcelona, having themselves become large landlords, tended to support the nobility in resisting the reduction of peasant taxes. Simultaneously, the decline of Barcelona's Mediterranean trade had made the merchant oligarchy increasingly tight-fisted in its relations with urban artisans and unskilled workmen.

The economic and social problems were complicated by dynastic and regional conflicts. In the 1460s, when, as has been seen (above p. 141), the merchant oligarchs of Barcelona rebelled against John II, they appealed to the populace on grounds of Catalan patriotism, and during the ensuing decade of civil war all social classes were divided over the regional question. Thus some landlords and their *remensa* enemies sided with the Aragonese monarch, while other landlords and poorer peasants opted for an independent Catalonia. Similarly, some merchants and artisans chose Catalan nationalism over their pragmatic interests; others favoured John II, on grounds of the national unity of Aragon-Catalonia and the intelligent economic policies of the king.

Castile as well as Aragon witnessed civil war in the 1460s. Peasants were conscious of landlord exactions, and the municipalities sought the aid of the king against a turbulent nobility. Farmers and townsmen alike offered violent resistance to the sheep-herders who encroached on their cultivated fields. They shared also an increasing suspicion and jealousy of the *conversos*, who were so prominent in the economy, and in high civil and ecclesiastical offices. Class lines were no more rigidly drawn than in the Catalan civil war, but in the struggle between the supporters of Henry IV and of his half-sister Isabella, it may be stated generally that the more pluralistic, tolerant forces favoured Henry, and, the more orthodox and traditionalist forces Isabella. Henry had a daughter Juana by his Portuguese queen, but a successful campaign of defamation had convinced many people that the king was impotent, and that the princess had been begotten by the royal favourite, D. Beltran de la Cueva. Isabella was hesitating between a Portuguese and an Aragonese marriage, and upon her choice might well depend

119, 120   The Catholic kings. Left, Ferdinand: detail of the High Altar attributed to Gil de Siloe. Isabella: a portrait attributed to Bartolome Bermejo.

the future orientation of Castile – towards the Atlantic or towards the Mediterranean. At the same time, however, her peaceable inheritance of the Castilian throne was by no means certain, nor could anyone know the extent of her political ability.

When in 1469 the headstrong princess Isabella married her cousin Ferdinand, neither party enjoyed a secure heritage. But in 1474 Isabella did inherit her brother's throne without violence, and in 1479 Ferdinand ascended his father's throne in Aragon-Catalonia. Suddenly it appeared that Castile and Aragon, which had been ruled separately for the previous five centuries, and which had been torn by civil war for much of the fifteenth century, would now at last become united under the Trastamara cousins.

Ferdinand and Isabella were both persons of outstanding intelligence. Ferdinand was crafty, cool and courageous, highly successful in his diplomatic dealings with European princes, and moderately successful as a military leader in the decade of war against Granada. He was neither sentimental nor idealistic. As a ruler concerned for the loyalty and prosperity of his subjects, he interested himself actively in justice, and in economic and financial regulations. Isabella had broader interests, in music and humanistic learning as well as in political and economic questions. But she was also a religious fanatic, and she shared the quasi-racist prejudices of her Old Christian subjects against Jews, *conversos* and Mudejars. Ferdinand held full authority in Aragon, and the two were co-sovereigns in Castile.

The overriding political aim of the two monarchs was to increase the authority and bolster the economic position of the crown. In Castile they destroyed the castles of the fractious nobility and reclaimed for the royal domain various lands and tax revenues which had been alienated by John II and Henry IV. They lessened their dependence upon the *conversos* by training a new class of civil servants, the so-called *letrados*, drawn con-

121 The Reconquest of Granada: a wall painting depicting a fight between Christian and Moor.

The Alcazar of Segovia; ...ere Ferdinand and Isabella were first proclaimed.

scientiously from Old Christian families. They supported the Santa Hermandad, a sort of federation of volunteer police forces which the municipalities had organized for their self-protection during the civil wars. Under Ferdinand and Isabella the activities of the Hermandad were directed by a royal appointee, the bishop of Cartagena, and taxes for its upkeep were paid by the clergy and the nobility as well as by the towns. The brotherhood pursued highway robbers, political dissidents and troublesome 'vagrants' of all sorts. For such crimes as arson, robbery and rebellion (the operative definitions of which it is difficult to pin down) they frequently inflicted the death penalty by a volley of arrows. They shared with Isabella the self-righteous emotions of the Old Christian farmers, artisans and soldiers – the 'forgotten men' of late medieval Spain. The queen used them in her struggle against the high nobility and also to intimidate the potentially 'disloyal' middle class, i.e. the Jews and *conversos*.

The Catholic kings also intended, by their economic measures, to encourage the development of the middle class. They unified weights and measures, and issued a reliable monetary unit, the *excelente*, equal in value to the Venetian ducat. They subsidized road and harbour improvement, and suppressed many internal tolls within their kingdoms. In order to encourage the textile industry, they decreed that only two-thirds of Spain's raw wool could be exported. However, in all direct conflicts between the interests of agriculture and those of sheep- and cattle-ranchers, they favoured the latter. They banned enclosures of new communal lands that had been opened to farming under Henry IV, and permitted deforestation so as to create new upland pastures. There were a number of traditional, unfenced sheepwalks criss-crossing all of Castile from the Cantabrican mountains to the Sierra Morena. Conflicts over the boundaries of these sheep-walks were settled in favour of the powerful ranchers' guild, the Mesta. Municipalities and hardy individuals were constantly complaining to the courts about invasions of their lands. A law of 1501 permitted the Mesta to retain any fields which it had used for grazing purposes for several months, even without the knowledge of the owners.

123 Sixteenth-century gold *excelente:* left, the crowned busts of Ferdinand and Isabella; the reverse side shows an eagle with the crowned shield of Leon and Castile.

: comer. beuer. calcar. uene. vibrar. consolar. enterrar.

124 Symbiosis of Jewish and Christian cultures. Rabbi Moses Arragel presents his Spanish translation of the Bible to the Grand Master of the order of Calatrava, Don Luis de Guzman.

Such bald favouritism towards the Mesta at the expense of Castilian agriculture was due in large part to the economic necessities of the crown itself. Through direct political pressures the queen had seen to it that Ferdinand was chosen grand master of each of the three great military orders as those masterships became vacant. The orders in turn were Spain's largest ranchers, and through control of them the crown received the enormous tax revenue collected from sheep-herders. At the same time two other traditional sources of revenue were failing to maintain their earlier importance. By the 1470s Sudanese gold, which had formerly reached the Castilian treasury via the tribute payments of Granada, was flowing to Portugal rather than Granada as a result of Portuguese enterprise in Africa. By the late fifteenth century the Portuguese had also cut heavily into Aragon's share of the spice trade. In the 1480s the sovereigns needed large new sums of money for their war against Granada. At the same time they did not want to increase taxes which

185

125 Bridge leading into a medieval city: detail from a fifteenth-century altarpiece.

126 Opposite, unloading cargo: detail from an altarpiece, attributed to Pedro Nisart.

would hurt the new metal or shipbuilding industries, nor would it have been politically feasible to increase local sales taxes. For all these reasons the crown depended more heavily than ever on the revenues from sheep-raising, and therefore favoured the interests of ranchers, regardless of the deleterious effects which might result in other branches of the economy.

It is a moot question whether Ferdinand and Isabella intended fully to unify the economies of Aragon and Castile. While suppressing many local tolls they did not eliminate the customs barriers between the two kingdoms. At harbour berths in Seville or Santander and at the great international fair in Medina del Campo, Catalan merchants were treated as foreigners. Genoese bankers were preponderant in Castilian finance, and the Genoese had been bitter rivals of the Catalans for centuries. In any event, only in the matter of currency was there a true economic unification of the two kingdoms. Nor did the Catholic kings break the economic power of the nobility. They enforced

their political authority, but at the close of their reign the nobility still owned or directly controlled 97 per cent of the soil of Spain, with some 45 per cent being held by bishoprics, cathedral chapters and city-dwelling nobles; and some 52 per cent belonging to large rural estates, the so-called *latifundia*. The general result of their policies was to confirm the power of that portion of the nobility which supported the crown politically, and to encourage the Old Christian elements of the middle class and farming population wherever those interests did not conflict with the interests of wool-producers.

Of the co-sovereigns Isabella was surely the more 'committed' in an ideological sense. Once she had ensured royal control of the nobility and had sensed the ground-swell of a public opinion grateful for her achievement of 'law and order' she was determined to complete the territorial reconquest of Spain and to rid both kingdoms of heretics and Jews. The final war against Granada occupied the entire decade between 1481 and 1491. The

army took the field each spring and autumn, conducting scorched-earth raids with some thirty thousand troops trained especially in the destruction of crops, grain-mills and water supplies. The hills of the kingdom of Granada were full of heavy stone fortresses, and the sovereigns imported German and Italian artillery specialists whose guns hurled larger metal and stone projectiles than had yet been employed in European warfare. The advance was slowed by the need for new roads and bridges to support the sheer weight of the artillery. The enthusiastic participation of the nobility was encouraged by the official papal bull of crusade, by sentiments of chivalry towards the great queen, and by ceremonial jousts and banquets during the long intervals between actual military campaigns.

Money was borrowed in large quantities from Italian and Flemish bankers abroad, and from Jews and *conversos* at home.

127 Opposite, Ferdinand attacks and takes Gor in 1489.

128, 129 Christian soldiers and Muslim warriors.

130 Helmet of Boabdil, last Moorish king of Granada.

The sovereigns offered generous terms of surrender, promising freedom of worship and the continuance of Muslim law in local government. Their practice was frequently anything but generous. During the three-month siege of Malaga in 1487 they burned numerous *conversos* and killed renegade Christians by the pointed reed torture. The Jewish royal financier, Abraham Senior, paid a ransom of 20,000 *doblas* to save four hundred and fifty Jews from being sold into African slavery. After the final capture of the city one-third of the population was exchanged for Christian captives held in North Africa, one-third was sold as slaves, and many hundreds were distributed to the nobility and to friendly sovereigns. One hundred converted Muslim warriors were sent to join the papal guard, fifty women were sent as a gift to the queen of Naples, and thirty to the queen of Portugal.

Granadan military resistance was often dogged and desperately courageous. Generous promises, cruel conduct, and the deportation and enslavement of whole populations were all common characteristics of the increasingly fanatical borderland and piratical encounters between the Christian and Muslim worlds in the late fifteenth century. Thus the Catholic kings could amply justify their own conduct by reference to the treatment of Christian captives in North Africa. Although the war dragged on for ten years, its outcome was never in serious doubt. The most serious logistic problem was how to pay the wages of the Spanish troops and the foreign specialists, and how to meet the costs of road- and bridge-building, siege warfare and royal jousts.

Queen Isabella found the perfect instrument for both her financial needs and her religious preoccupations in founding an institution which was destined to play an immense role in the Hispanic world for three centuries to come: the Spanish Inquisition. The operation and significance of inquisitorial courts – courts which tested religious orthodoxy by means of secret testimony and torture – was well known in fifteenth-century Spain. In the first decades of the thirteenth century, a papal inquisition, staffed largely by Dominican friars, had been instrumental in suppressing the Albigensian heresy in Languedoc. Many refugees from that religious persecution had settled in Aragon, and the papal inquisition had also operated in the latter kingdom. But the kings of Aragon in the thirteenth century, and for the two following centuries, consistently resisted the inquisition in favour of pursuing tolerant policies towards Jews, Muslims, and the converts of both religions.

In Castile there had been no reason to establish an inquisition until after the period of mass conversions between 1391 and 1416. D. Alvaro de Luna, the *converso* favourite of John II, had thought of using an inquisition to destroy the power of the many *conversos* whom he saw as leagued with the nobility in opposition to his own power. In 1451 he applied to the pope, Nicholas V, for a grant of inquisitorial power. Papal consent came just after the fall of Luna in 1453, and neither the succeeding king, Henry IV, nor his main supporters, cared to make use of the grant. One of those who was most disappointed at this inaction was the *converso* Franciscan friar Alonso de Espina, who wrote and distributed anti-Jewish tracts from his office as rector of the university of Salamanca.

Shortly after her accession in 1474, Isabella was urged by pope Sixtus IV to establish a papal inquisition in Castile. She and her consort Ferdinand countered by making secret application in 1478 for a Castilian inquisition. Negotiations proceeded for several months, at the end of which the pope conceded full royal control not only of the new inquisition, but also of the nominations to bishoprics in Castile. Publication of the news dumbfounded the large and well-to-do *converso* community of Seville. Many municipal councillors sought refuge on the estates of friendly nobles, thereby increasing the queen's suspicions regarding the loyalty of both the refugees and their hosts. A minor outbreak of plague helped to prepare public opinion for a wave of burnings.

The first *auto da fé* took place in Seville in February 1481, and altogether, according to Isabella's court chronicler, the *converso*

131   Heretics at the stake: detail from *Auto da Fé*, attributed to Pedro Berruguete.

Hernando de Pulgar, some two thousand *converso* heretics were burned during the 1480s. Arrests were made in secret, if possible. Families were warned to say nothing, and the suspect's property was immediately sequestered, thereby becoming available to pay the costs of the inquisition and to subsidize the Granadan war. Victims were urged to make full confessions of their own judaizing activities, and to name all their acquaintances who might conceivably have engaged in similar acts. Pleas of insanity, or of the absence of heretical intent, were tested by torture, as was also the completeness of the main confession. The names of hostile witnesses were kept secret, and there was of course no right of cross-examination. The evidence of relatives was used against the defendant, but could not be cited on his behalf. Jews, Muslims and personal servants could not testify to the suspect's innocence, and if he were released, he was solemnly reprimanded for having attracted the attention of informers in the first place. The royal inquisition operated almost as a state within a state. Inquisitors were entitled to free lodging, were exempt from local taxes and from the jurisdiction of both secular and ecclesiastical courts. Taken together, their secrecy, their autonomy, their royal patronage and their appeal to the worst prejudices of the ignorant and superstitious terrorized all those who could not be completely certain of their religious orthodoxy and their Old Christian lineage. The atmosphere of Seville in the 1480s was comparable only with that of Nazi Germany, or of Soviet Russia during the Stalinist blood-purges.

The inquisition, since it applied specifically to the *conversos*, had the unintended effect of slowing down the process of conversion among the Spanish Jews. But for the leading inquisitors, many of whom, like Torquemada, were themselves *conversos*, the Jews were the great enemy, and their political problem was how to connect the Jews inescapably with the crimes of the *conversos*. In June 1490, one Benito Garcia, who had been a Christian for thirty-five years, was arrested in Astorga on his way home from a pilgrimage to Santiago. His examiners found a consecrated wafer in his knapsack. In the course of six days' torture, he named five *conversos* and two Jews as his confederates in the ritual murder of a Christian child. He confessed that, by magical use of the child's heart and the consecrated wafer, they intended to cause all Christians to die insane and the Jews to obtain their wealth. No child had been reported missing in the village of La Guardia, nor was one ever found, but the Dominican friar and inquisitor-general Thomas Torquemada gave great publicity to the allegations, and by the autumn of 1491 a cult of the Holy Child of La Guardia was being celebrated. (Interested tourists may still see the hermitage near Ocaña, south of Madrid.)

Torquemada seized upon this incident to urge upon the sovereigns the necessity of exiling the Jews from their dominions. During the Granadan war they had borrowed money from Jews and used Jewish tax-farmers, as had all the preceding kings of Aragon and Castile. They had also, like their predecessors, published restrictive decrees which were only half-heartedly applied in practice. It was therefore almost impossible for the Jews to believe, when Isabella signed the decrees offering conversion or expulsion as the only alternatives, that the end had really come. They tried once more, as on past occasions, to substitute a money ransom for the stark decree. But the queen, who knew her own mind, and had just completed the reconquest of Granada, insisted on literal application. Ferdinand gave his consent as co-sovereign in Castile, but the Jews were not officially expelled from Aragon until his grandson, the emperor Charles V, had mounted the throne.

It has always been difficult for rational men, and for admirers of queen Isabella's many excellent qualities as a ruler, to understand why she chose, in the years of her greatest power and prosperity, to destroy tens of thousands of the most valuable of Castile's human resources. One simple, and important, explanation is that she was indeed a bigot who included the notion of racial purity among her reasons. She was also perfectly well aware of the economic and social effects of her policies. Thus,

132   Gil de Siloe's sculpture in Burgos cathedral depicts, in the manner of traditional Christian iconography, the Jewish faith blindfolded and worldly; Christianity, by contrast, is chastely dressed and can see the truth.

answering criticisms of the inquisition which had impressed the pope himself, she wrote to her papal ambassador as follows: 'I have caused great calamities and depopulated towns, lands, provinces, and kingdoms, but I have acted thus from love of Christ and His Holy Mother. Those are liars and calumniators who say I have done so for love of money, for I have never myself touched a *maravedi* from the confiscated goods of the dead. On the contrary I have employed the money in educating and giving marriage portions to the children of the condemned.'

But it would be foolish to attribute to one ruler's personal emotions a series of actions so significant as the establishment of the Holy Office and the expulsion of the Jews. Anti-semitism had been rising in Spain from the time of the Black Death in the mid-fourteenth century. The events of the years between 1391 and 1416 had created the *converso* problem without 'solving' the Jewish question. Throughout the fifteenth century the 'common man' in Castile had increasingly identified the Jews and the *conversos* with the hated nobility. In a massive backlash against the great economic and cultural influence of the *conversos*, public opinion had applauded the anti-semitic Hermandad and the anti-semitic queen. For the Old Christians the financial shakedown of the *converso* community to pay for the Granadan war, and the expulsion of the Jews with the requirement that they leave their valuables behind, were well-justified ways of restoring to Castile what the Jews and *conversos* had robbed from her over several centuries.

Thinking more broadly of the entire experience of the Middle Ages, a sovereign of Castile or Aragon might well have asked himself the following question: was it possible to take the extremely varied human material of Spain and weld it into one nation? Could one hope to have laws and customs equally valid for Castilian shepherds and soldiers, for Cantabrican and Andalusian sailors, for Mudejar farmers and artisans, for Jewish and *converso* financiers, doctors, cartographers? The answer would seem to have been, not only for Isabella, but also for her successors until the late eighteenth century: perhaps, but only on the basis of strict religious unity. In Spain of the sixteenth, seventeenth and eighteenth centuries racial prejudice was only an occasional and subordinate factor. But sovereign after sovereign doubted the loyalty of converted Jews and converted Muslims, and was willing to sacrifice the economic and intellectual interests of Spain to the overriding need for religious orthodoxy as a test of political reliability. The emirs and caliphs of the ninth and tenth centuries, and the Christian kings of the thirteenth to the mid-fifteenth, had tried to establish pluralistic régimes with three recognized religious communities owing loyalty to a single dynastic sovereign. But these efforts had foundered in civil wars and in revolutions of rising expectations, whether in eleventh-century al-Andalus or in fifteenth-century Castile and Aragon. It thus seemed that Spain could be governed peaceably only on the basis of religious unity.

The year 1492 was indeed a fateful one in the history of Castile. Simultaneously she completed the reconquest, expelled the Jews and discovered America. She drastically contracted her economic and intellectual resources just at the moment when she was about to become a world power. She resolutely turned her back on the ideal of cultural pluralism at the very moment when she was about to extend her rule over Red men of greatly varied cultures. Fortunately for mankind the rulers of Spain did not succeed in imposing the kind of religious and intellectual conformity which they sought. With the means of physical coercion and intellectual control available before the twentieth century it was not possible to contain the cultural energies of a great people. *Converso* friars and businessmen flourished in the New World, far from the centres of imposed orthodoxy. Within Spain itself, Christians both Old and New resisted the spirit of the inquisition and created heterodox currents which maintained much of the medieval pluralism. And the very tension between the forces of repression and prejudice on the one hand, and the open, candid, joyous, energetic way of life of the Spanish people on the other, helped to create the literary and artistic glories of Spain's Golden Age.

BIBLIOGRAPHY

Most of the important scholarship relating to medieval Spain has been written by Spanish and French authors, but for the convenience of English-language readers I will discuss first the authoritative works available in English. Two general histories which contain valuable chapters on the Middle Ages are Rafael Altamira, *A History of Spain* (D. Van Nostrand Co., New York 1949), and Harold Livermore, *A History of Spain* (Allen and Unwin, 2nd ed. London 1966). Altamira was the dean of Spanish historians during the first third of the present century; his judgments are broadminded and temperate. Livermore is particularly useful for concise, accurate summaries of political and institutional matters. J. Vicens Vives and J. Nadal Oller, *An Economic History of Spain* (Princeton University Press, 1969), is a fine translation of the only reliable general study of Spanish economic history. Roger B. Merriman, *The Rise of the Spanish Empire* vol. I, 'The Middle Ages' (Macmillan, New York 1918), remains very useful for institutional and dynastic history. A. R. Nykl, *Hispano-Arabic Poetry and its Relations with the Old Provençal Troubadours* (J. H. Furst Co., Baltimore 1946), contains valuable translations and historical notes even if the validity of the thesis as suggested by his title is questionable. James T. Monroe, *The Risála of Ibn García and Five Refutations* (University of California Press, 1969), highlights the ethnic conflicts of the *taifa* period. A. A. Neuman, *The Jews in Spain . . . During the Middle Ages* (2 vols., Philadelphia 1921), and Yitzhak Baer, *A History of the Jews in Christian Spain* (2 vols., Philadelphia 1961 and 1966), are both magnificent works of scholarship issued by the Jewish Publication Society of America. Américo Castro, *The Structure of Spanish History* (Princeton University Press, 1954), relies too heavily on purely literary sources and overstates its valuable analyses of Islamic and Hebrew influences. H. J. Chaytor, *A History of Aragon and Catalonia* (Methuen, London 1933), is very useful on political and institutional questions, and Evelyn S. Procter, *Alfonso X of Castile* (Clarendon Press, Oxford 1951), emphasizes cultural contributions. Robert I. Burns, *The Crusader*

Kingdom of Valencia (Harvard University Press, 2 vols., 1967), emphasizes the problems of the thirteenth-century frontier between Christian and Muslim Spain, and Thomas F. Glick, in *Irrigation and Society in Medieval Valencia* (Harvard University Press, 1970), studies in detail the famous water tribunals. Julius Klein, *The Mesta* (Harvard University Press, 1920), studies the economic power of the sheep- and cattle-ranchers. Henry C. Lea, *A History of the Inquisition of Spain* (Macmillan, 4 vols., New York 1906–7), is a classic of both research and interpretation. Henry Kamen, *The Spanish Inquisition* (Weidenfeld and Nicolson, London 1965), is an excellent recent study. Jacques Lassaigne, *Spanish Painting from the Catalan Frescoes to El Greco* (Editions A. Skira, Geneva 1962), contains both beautiful colour reproductions and valuable commentary.

Two very short, brilliant interpretations of Spanish history as a whole which have recently become available in English are Pierre Vilar, *Spain, a Brief History* (Pergamon, Oxford 1967), and J. Vicens Vives, *Approaches to the History of Spain* (University of California Press, 1967).

The best available general history of the Spanish Middle Ages until 1212 is Luis G. de Valdeavellano, *Historia de España* (Revista de Occidente, 2 vols., Madrid 1955). Valuable also for their numerous illustrations, detailed footnotes and special emphasis on Aragon-Catalonia are the first two volumes of Ferran Soldevila, *Historia de España* (Ediciones Ariel, Barcelona 1959 and 1962). In the multi-volume collective work edited by R. Menéndez Pidal, *Historia de España* (Espasa Calpe, Madrid 1947), vols. IV and V, 'España musulmana 711–1031' are a translation, with excellent notes and illustrations, of E. Lévi-Provençal, *Histoire de l'Espagne Musulmane* (Paris-Leyden 1950–53). Volume VI, 'España Cristiana, 711–1038' is strongest on political and religious history. R. P. Dozy, *Histoire des Musulmans d'Espagne* (edited by Lévi-Provençal, Leyden 1932), remains the most satisfactory general work on Muslim Spain, combining the virtues of the great Dutch scholar's insight and enthusiasm with the more careful critical approach to sources of his French disciple. Other works of great value on the Islamic period are: Henri Pérès, *La poésie andalouse en arabe classique* (Adrien-Maisonneuve, Paris 1953); E. García Gómez, *Poemas arábigo-andaluces* (Editorial Plutarco, Madrid 1930); A. Prieto Vives, *Los reyes de taifa* (Centro de Estudios Históricos, Madrid 1926); Henri Terrasse, *Islam d'Espagne* (Plon, Paris 1958).

Claudio Sánchez-Albornoz, *España, un enigma histórico* (Editorial Sudamericana, 2 vols., Buenos Aires 1962), and *Estudios sobre las instituciones medievales españolas* (Mexico, D.F. 1965) are indispensable both for data and interpretation, though the former work is marred by anti-Semitic innuendos. Aly Mazahéri, *La vie quotidienne des musulmans au moyen age* (Hachette, Paris 1951); I. de las Cagigas, *Los mozárabes* (Escelier, 2 vols., Madrid 1948), and *Los mudéjares* (Escelier, 2 vols., Madrid 1949); and Marcel Defourneaux, *Les français en Espagne aux xie et xiie siècles* (Presses Universitaires de France, Paris 1949), contain useful information on the various religious and national groups.

Particularly important for understanding various aspects of the reconquest are R. Menéndez Pidal, *La España del Cid* (Editorial Plutarco, Madrid 1929, with numerous revised editions, and an English translation by H. Sunderland, *The Cid and his Spain*, John Murray, London 1934); J.M. Lacarra (editor) *La reconquista española y la repoblación del país* (Zaragoza 1951); Julio González, *Repartimiento de Sevilla* (2 vols., Madrid 1951); and A. Huici Miranda, *Las grandes batallas de la reconquista durante las invasiones africanas* (Instituto de Estudios Africanos, Madrid 1956). A pioneer work on the governing institutions of Aragon is Ludwig Klüpfel, *Verwaltungsgeschichte des Königreichs Aragon zu Ende des 13. Jahrhunderts* (Kohlhammer, Berlin 1915). Recent groundbreaking studies in economic history are A. Masiá de Ros, *La corona de Aragón y los estados del norte de Africa* (Barcelona 1951), and C. E. Dufourcq, *L'Espagne catalane et le Maghrib aux xiiie et xive siècles* (Presses Universitaires de France, Paris 1966). Important works on medieval Spanish art are: Juan de Contreras, Marqués de Lozoya, *Historia del arte hispanico*, vol. 2 (Salvat Editores, Barcelona 1935); E. Camps Cazorla, *El arte románico en España* (Editorial Labor, Barcelona 1935); and Henri Terrasse, *L'Espagne du moyen age* (Fayard, Paris 1966). Fundamental to an understanding of the social revolutions of the fifteenth century and the background to the triumphs of Ferdinand and Isabella are four works by the late J. Vicens Vives: *Juan II de Aragón* (Barcelona 1953), *Historia crítica de la vida y reinado de Fernando II de Aragón* (Zaragoza 1961), *Historia de los remensas en el siglo XV* (Instituto "Jerónimo Zurita", Barcelona 1945), and *El siglo XV, Els Trastàmares* (Teide, Barcelona 1956); and Orestes Ferrara, *L'avènement d'Isabelle la Catholique* (Albin Michel, Paris 1958), a slight revision of the original study published in Spanish as *Un pleito sucesorio* (Madrid 1945). Many fundamental studies have only appeared in learned journals, the most indispensable of which are *Al-Andalus* (Madrid), *Bulletin Hispanique* (Bordeaux), *Hispania* (Madrid), *Spanische Forschungen der Görres Gesellschaft* (Münster, Westfalen) and *Cuadernos de Historia de España* (Buenos Aires).

Finally, it should be noted that several of the scholars named above have written numerous other books and articles, all of which deserve the attention of any reader interested in medieval Spain: Américo Castro, J.M. Lacarra, E. Lévi-Provençal, Ramón Menéndez Pidal, Claudio Sánchez-Albornoz, Ferran Soldevila and J. Vicens Vives.

RULERS OF THE PERIOD

KINGS OF ASTURIAS		KINGS OF LEON		UMAYYAD RULERS OF CORDOBA	
Alfonso I	739–57	Ordoño II (son of Alfonso III)	914–24	Abd-al-Rahman I	756–88
Fruela	757–68	Ramiro II	931–51	Hisham I	788–96
Alfonso II (El Casto)	791–842	Ordoño III	951–56	al-Hakam I	796–822
Ramiro I	842–50	Sancho I	956–66	Abd-al-Rahman II	822–52
Ordoño I	850–66			Muhammad I	852–86
Alfonso III (El Magno)	866–910	Fernan Gonzalez	c. 910–70	al-Mundhir	886–88
		(count of Castile)		Abdallah	888–912
				Abd-al-Rahman III	912–61
				al-Hakam II	961–76
				Hisham II	976–1009
				al-Mansur	c. 967–1002
				(dictator in Cordoba)	
				Taifa kings	1009–90
				Almoravids	1090–1147
				Almohads	1147–1212

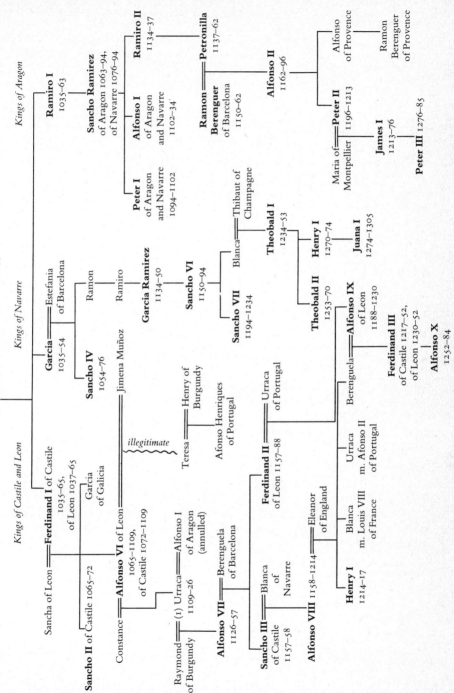

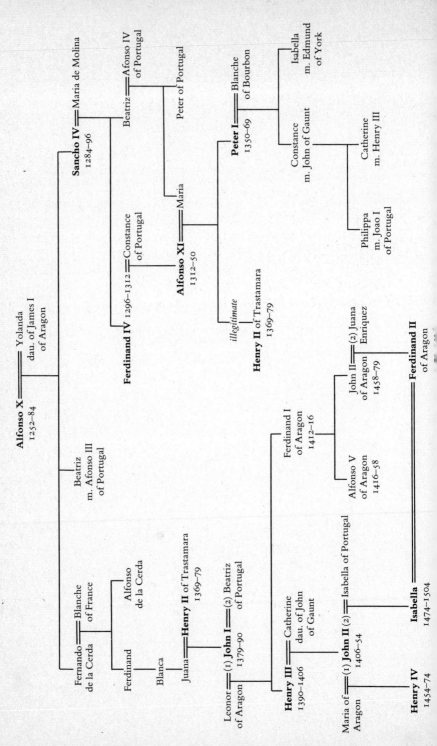

THE HOUSE OF CASTILE (1252–1504)

THE HOUSE OF ARAGON (1276–1516)

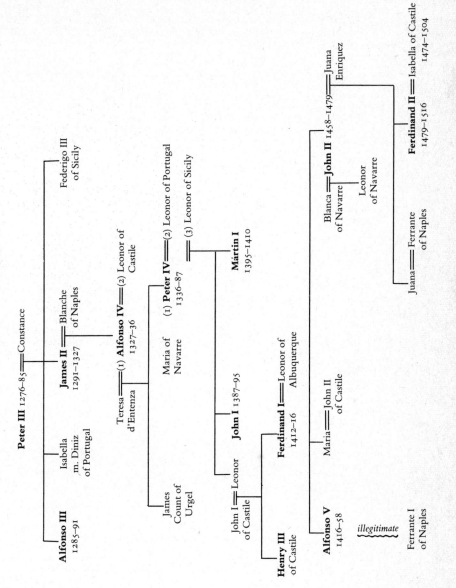

Peter III 1276–85 ══ Constance

Alfonso III 1285–91

Isabella m. Diniz of Portugal

James II 1291–1327 ══ Blanche of Naples

Federigo III of Sicily

Teresa d'Entenza ══(1) **Alfonso IV** 1327–36 ══(2) Leonor of Castile

James Count of Urgel

Maria of Navarre (1) **Peter IV** 1336–87 ══(2) Leonor of Portugal

══(3) Leonor of Sicily

Mártin I 1395–1410

John I ══ Leonor of Castile

John I 1387–95

Ferdinand I 1412–16 ══ Leonor of Albuquerque

Henry III of Castile

Maria ══ John II of Castile

Alfonso V 1416–58

illegitimate

Ferrante I of Naples

Juana ══ Ferrante of Naples

Blanca ══ **John II** 1458–1479 ══ Juana Enriquez

Leonor of Navarre

Ferdinand II 1479–1516 ══ Isabella of Castile 1474–1504

LIST OF ILLUSTRATIONS

207

49 Statuette of Ferdinand III of Castile as a Holy Knight; fifteenth century. Kunstversteigerungshaus Weinmüller, Munich

50 Seal of James I of Aragon-Catalonia showing the king enthroned. Archivo de la Ciudad, Barcelona. Photo: Mas

51 Detail of an altarpiece of St George showing the intervention of St George on behalf of James I of Aragon-Catalonia in the battle against the Moors beneath the walls of Majorca (1230): the altarpiece, commissioned in 1468, is attributed to Pedro Nisart. Museo Diocesano, Palma de Mallorca. Photo: Mas

52 Detail of a wall painting showing James I of Aragon-Catalonia and his soldiers entering Valencia in triumph (1238); late thirteenth century or early fourteenth century. Castel d'Alcanyís. Photo: Mas.

53 Detail of a wall painting showing Catalan knights; Catalan school; late thirteenth century or early fourteenth century. Tinell de Barcelona. Photo: Mas

54 Detail of a wall painting showing Catalan archers; Catalan school; late thirteenth century or early fourteenth century. Tinell de Barcelona. Photo: Mas

55 Map of the thirteenth-century Reconquest. Drawn by Shalom Schotten

56 Miniature showing the banquet held at Tarragona for James I of Aragon-Catalonia and his nobles by the citizen of Barcelona, Pedro Martell, captain of the galleys; the king sits alone at a separate table while a kneeling cup-bearer serves him drinks; 1343; from the *Libre del Feyts de Jaume I*, fol. 27r. Biblioteca de la Universidad, Barcelona. Photo: Mas

57 Miniature of a country scene with a peasant making spoons and another with a donkey; from a manuscript of the *Natural History* by Albertus Magnus; fourteenth century. Biblioteca de la Universidad, Granada. Photo: Mas

58 Miniature showing a king receiving the homage of his vassals, from the *Libro Verde*; late fourteenth century. Museo de Historia de la Ciudad, Barcelona. Photo: Mas

59 Miniature of a peasant ploughing, from a Spanish manuscript of the works of Virgil, frontispiece of the *Georgics*; fifteenth century. Biblioteca de la Universidad, Valencia. Photo: Mas

60 Miniature of a country scene showing peasants ploughing, pruning, dairy-farming and bee-keeping, from a Spanish manuscript of the works of Virgil, frontispiece of the *Georgics*; fifteenth century. Biblioteca de la Universidad, Valencia. Photo: Mas

61 Detail of an altarpiece of St Margherita showing sheep grazing; Catalan school; fifteenth century. Museo Diocesano, Vic

62 Exterior façade of the house built by Samuel Abulafia in Toledo; it is fortified and almost without windows. Photo: Mas

63 Jew wearing the badge of the Jew on his chest, detail of a wall painting; fourteenth century. Transept, Tarragona Cathedral. Photo: Mas

64 Miniature showing a Passover service in a Jewish home; from a Hebrew manuscript of the Domestic Passover service written in a Spanish hand; fourteenth century. MS Or. 2884, fol. 18r. Courtesy Trustees of the British Museum, London

65 Tables and figures of the constellation of the Bear, from the Astronomical Tables of Peter IV; fourteenth century. Hebrew MS 132, fol. 66r. Nationalbibliothek, Vienna

66 *Tablas Alfonsinas* – reliquary triptych; thirteenth century. Seville Cathedral. Photo: Mas

67 Marble capital from Medinat al-Zahira, near Cordoba. Courtesy the Victoria and Albert Museum, London

68 Interior view of San Miguel de Escalada, province of Leon, consecrated in 913. Photo: Hirmer Fotoarchiv

69 Cloister of the monastery of Santa Maria de Ripoll, province of Gerona. Photo: Hirmer Fotoarchiv

70 Nave of the abbey church, Meira, province of Galicia. Bibliothèque Nationale, Paris

71 Romanesque doors of the abbey church, Meira, province of Galicia. Bibliothèque Nationale, Paris

Portico of San Lorenzo de Carboeiro, Galicia; Cistercian; eleventh to twelfth century. Photo: Author

Santa Maria de Ripoll, Gerona; sculptured west façade of the main portal; *c.* 1125–50. Photo: Hirmer Fotoarchiv

Tower and abside of San Lorenzo, Sahagun; Mudejar; thirteenth century. Photo: Author

Main façade of the Alcazar, Seville; the present building is mainly the work of Christian kings, especially Peter the Cruel, but it is built in the Moorish style, probably by Moorish builders. Photo: Mas

Miniature from the *Libro del Consulado del Mar* (1409) attributed to Domingo Crespi. Photo: Mas

Stylized portraits of Ramon Berenguer IV of Barcelona and Petronilla, his betrothed; miniature from the genealogical tree of Poblet, *c.* 1395–1409. Monastery of Poblet, Tarragona. Photo: Mas

Tomb of Peter III of Aragon, late thirteenth century. Santa Cruz, Tarragona. Photo: Mas

Miniature showing a sailing ship; a friar among the passengers holds a picture of the Virgin and Child to protect the ship; to the right is a view of a town; miniature of *Las Cantigas de Santa Maria*, Cant. XXXV. Real Biblioteca de San Lorenzo de El Escorial, Madrid. Photo: Mas

Detail of the map of Spain made by the Jewish cartographer Iresques of Majorca in 1375; Granada bears an Arabic emblem indicating that it is still Muslim; Toledo is represented as entirely surrounded by water. Bibliothèque Nationale, Paris.

Seal of James II of Aragon-Catalonia; inscribed: SIGILLUM IACOBI DEI GRACIA REGIS ARAGONUM, VALENCIE, SARDINIE ET CORSICE AC COMITIS BARCHINONE. Photo: Mas

Map of the economic and artistic life of Spain. Drawn by Shalom Schotten

Statues believed to be of Alfonso X of Castile and queen Violante; French school, *c.* 1275. Cathedral cloister, Burgos. Photo: Mas

Miniature showing a game of chess in a pharmacy, medicine jars stand on shelves at the back of the shop; from the Chess Book of Alfonso X of Castile (known as 'the Wise'); late thirteenth century. MS T, I, 6, fol. 31r. Real Biblioteca de San Lorenzo de El Escorial, Madrid. Photo: Mas

85 Miniature showing Sancho IV of Castile and his attendants and the archbishop and his clergy in the cathedral of Toledo; from the *Privilegium Sanchos IV*, 1285; MS VIT, 14–138. Archivo Historico Nacional, Madrid. Photo: Mas

86 Portraits of Henry IV of Castile and other members of the house of Trastamara, from the *Geneaology of the Kings of Spain* by Alfonso de Cartagena; fifteenth century. Palacio Real, Madrid. Photo: Mas

87 Portraits of John I of Castile and other members of the house of Trastamara; John I is shown trodden under by his horse: possibly a reference to his defeat at the battle of Aljubarrota against the Portuguese in 1385; from the *Geneaology of the Kings of Spain* by Alfonso de Cartagena; fifteenth century. Palacio Real, Madrid. Photo: Mas

88 Portrait of Henry later Henry IV of Castile (known as 'the Impotent'); his armour, and especially his helmet, is characteristically foppish; his horse tramples on Moorish heads: a reference to the persecution of the Moors which was under way in his reign and which broke out in full fury under his successor; from the *Geneaology of the Kings of Spain* by Alfonso de Cartagena; fifteenth century. Palacio Real, Madrid. Photo: Mas

89 Statue in painted alabaster now believed to represent Peter IV of Aragon; attributed to Jaime Castells; fourteenth century. Formerly it was thought to be an effigy of Charlemagne and became an object of veneration until the cult was forbidden by Rome. Chapter room, Gerona Cathedral. Photo: Mas

90 Miniature showing James I of Majorca enthroned beneath a canopy being crowned by two angels; laymen and clerics surround the throne; beneath, Romeu des Paol is shown writing; from the *Privilegis dels Reis de Mallorca* (fol. 2r.); 1334. Archivo Historico, Palma de Mallorca. Photo: Mas

91 Martin I of Aragon; from a genealogical table of the early fifteenth century; MS Rothschild, 2529, fol. 28r. Bilbliothèque Nationale, Paris

92 Lead medal of Alfonso V of Aragon by Pisanello dated 1449; this type of medal was fashionable in the courts of the Italian princes at the time Alphonso was living in Naples. National Gallery of Art, Washington, D.C. (Kress Collection)

93 Miniature showing friars in attendance at the bier of a king, from a Liber Regalis; fourteenth to fifteenth century. Archivo de Navarra, Pamplona. Photo: Mas

94 Miniature of John II of Aragon with his coat of arms and the legend (in German): 'Hans, by God's grace King of Navarre and of Aragon, Duke of Venion and of Munblanck, Count of Ribbagorsa, Lord of the town of Baleager' from the diary of the German traveller Jörg von Ehingen; late fifteenth century. Historia 4 to. n. 141. Hauptstaatsarchiv, Stuttgart

95 Miniature of Carlos, prince of Viana, from the Letters of Ferdinand Bolea to the kings of Aragon, Castile and Portugal (fol. Ir.); fifteenth century. Biblioteca Nacional, Madrid. Photo: Mas

96 Miniature of scenes from the life of Ramon Llull. MS St Peter perg. 92, fol. 3v. Badische Landesbibliothek, Karlsruhe

97 Miniature showing Ildefonso of Toledo (a seventh-century bishop remembered for his opposition to those who doubted Mary's virginity) disputing with Jews; thirteenth century. MS T, I, I, fol. 7r. Real Biblioteca de San Lorenzo de El Escorial, Madrid

98 Interior of the synagogue built by Samuel Halevi, treasurer of Peter IV of Aragon shortly before his death (c. 1360); the style of the decoration is Mudejar-andaluz. Toledo. Photo: Mas

99 St Vincent Ferrer praying: detail of the altarpiece of the Virgin with St Vincent and donors attributed variously to Jaime Baço, called Jacomart, or his circle, to Pedro Huguet or to Pedro Garcia de Benabarre; fifteenth century. Musée des Arts Décoratifs, Paris

100 Jews wearing the badge of the Jew (a circle) on their hoods: detail of a capital. The third and fourth Lateran councils decreed that all Jews be obliged to wear the badge so that Christians could recognize and avoid them. Cloisters of Barcelona cathedral. Photo: Mas

101 Minstrels: detail of a capital; twelfth century. Cloister of the monastery of Santa Maria de L'Estany, Barcelona. Photo: Mas

102 Earliest extant manuscript of the Poem of the Cid, written by Pedro Abad in 1307 (i.e. two centuries after the death of Rodrigo Diaz, the Cid). Biblioteca Nacional, Madrid. Photo: Mas

103 Circular bowl decorated with dancing figures; early fourteenth century. Museo de Artes Decorativas, Barcelona. Photo: Mas

104 Portrait of the marques de Santillana, detail of the altarpiece of the marques by J. Inglés. Collection of the Duke of l'Infantado, Madrid. Photo: Mas

105 Nobleman hawking: detail from an altarpiece of St Bartholomew, school of Tarragona; c. 1360. Chapel of Corpus Christi, Tarragona Cathedral. Photo: Mas

106 Manuscript page of poetry by Auzias March; Spanish MS 225, fol. 28r. Bibliothèque Nationale, Paris.

107 Detail of a fresco by the Master of Pedret; late eleventh century. Santa Maria de Esterri d'Aneu, province of Lerida. Photo: Hirmer Fotoarchiv

108 The bulls of Tahull: detail of fresco in the apse of San Clemente de Tahull; Catalan school; c. 1123. Photo: Hirmer Fotoarchiv

109 Christ in glory: detail of fresco in the apse of San Clemente de Tahull; Catalan school; c. 1123. Photo: Hirmer Fotoarchiv

110 Detail of The Adoration of the Magi attributed to Ferrer Bassa; thirteenth-century wall painting in the Convent of the Nuns of St Clare Pedralbes, Barcelona

111 Detail of Pentecost attributed to Ferrer Bassa; thirteenth-century wall painting in the Monasterio de Pedralbes, Barcelona

112 Detail of St Peter Walking on the Water by Luis Borrassa. The Rector's House, Tarassa

3 Triptych of *Nativity* attributed to the Master of Avila. Lazaro Collection, Madrid. Photo: Mas

4 *The Devout before the tomb of St Vincent* attributed to Jaime Huguet; (detail). Museo de Arte de Cataluña, Barcelona. Photo: Mas

5 Detail of singing angels from the *Virgin of the Councillors* attributed to Luis Dalmau. Museo de Arte de Cataluña, Barcelona. Photo: Mas

6 *Christ in Majesty* attributed to Fernando Gallego. Museo del Prado, Madrid. Photo: Mas

7 *Pietà* attributed to Bartolome Bermejo. Barcelona Cathedral. Photo: Mas

8 *The Arrest of Santa Engracia* by Bartolome Bermejo. Fine Arts Gallery of San Diego, gift of Misses Anne R. and Amy Putnam, 1941

9 Portrait of Ferdinand of Aragon: detail of the marble High Altar attributed to Gil de Siloe. Cartija de Miraflores. Photo: Mas

10 Portrait of Isabella of Castile attributed to Bartolome Bermejo. Palacio Real, Madrid. Photo: Mas

11 Detail of a wall painting showing a fight between a Christian soldier and a Moorish warrior; fourteenth or fifteenth century. Sala de los Reyes, Alhambra, Granada. Photo: Mas

12 Castle of Segovia; originally an Arab stronghold; rebuilt by Henry IV and used by the court; Ferdinand and Isabella were proclaimed there. Photo: Mas

13 Gold *excelente*. Obverse: Crowned busts of Ferdinand and Isabella facing each other, inscribed: FERNANDUS ET ELISABET D.G. REX ET R. Reverse: Eagle with crowned shield of Leon and Castile quartering Aragon and Sicily; in the field to the right: T; to the left: five pellets inscribed: SUB UMBRA ALARUM TUARUM PROTEG[E]. National Gallery of Art, Washington, D.C. (Kress Collection)

14 Miniature showing Rabbi Moses Arragel presenting his Spanish translation of the Bible to his liege lord, Don Luis de Guzman, Grand Master of the order of Calatrava; knights of the order, each wearing his cross stand on either side; In the background, the knights feed ('comer'), give drink ('bever'), shoe ('calcar'), clothe ('vestir'), visit the sick ('visitar'), comfort ('consolar') and bury ('enterrar') Jews; a Dominican and Franciscan friar contemplate the scene; detail from the miniature in the Alba Bible showing the grand master on his throne (fol. 25v.); fifteenth century. Collection of the Duke of Alba, Madrid. Photo: Mas

125 View of a bridge leading into a medieval city, detail from the altarpiece of St Sebastian attributed to Rafael Vergos and Pedro Alemany; fifteenth century. Barcelona Cathedral. Photo: Mas

126 View of sailors unloading cargo, detail from the altarpiece of St George attributed to Pedro Nisart (*c.* 1468). Museo Diocesano, Palma de Mallorca. Photo: Mas

127 Carving in relief on a wooden choir-stall showing the attack on Gor by Ferdinand of Aragon in 1489; the town is well fortified; two Christian soldiers attack three Moors (left); Spanish troops enter the city gate, while a Moor shows the key above it; a pig and a monkey chant the Office (top left and right). The choir-stall was made by a German craftsman at the order of archbishop Pedro de Mendoza; *c.* 1489. Toledo Cathedral. Photo: Mas

128 Christian soldiers, detail from the altarpiece of St George attributed to Pedro Nisart (*c.* 1468). Museo Diocesano, Palma de Mallorca. Photo: Mas

129 Muslim warriors, detail from the Crucifixion in the altarpiece of Sant Miquel de Cruilles attributed to Luis Borrassa. Museo Diocesano, Gerona. Photo: Mas

130 Helmet of Boabdil, last Moorish king of Granada. Armería Real, Madrid. Photo: Mas

131 Condemned heretics being led to the stake, detail from *Auto da Fé* attributed to Berruguete. Museo del Prado, Madrid. Photo: Mas

132 Statues of the Church and the Synagogue by Gil de Siloe. Chapel of St Anne, Burgos Cathedral. Photo: Mas

INDEX

212